SURVIVAL SKILLS FOR SUPERVISORS AND MANAGERS

GUIDELINES FOR BUSINESS SUCCESS

ROBERTA CAVA

Survival Skills for Supervisors and Managers

Guidelines for business success

Roberta Cava

Published by Cava Consulting

cavaconsulting@ozemail.com.au

Discover other titles by Roberta Cava at
www.dealingwithdifficultpeople.info

National Library of Australia
Cataloguing-in-publication data:

ISBN 9780992340254

BOOKS BY ROBERTA CAVA

All can be purchased from Amazon Books
Non-Fiction

Dealing with Difficult People
(International best-seller since 1990 with 24 publishers – in 18
languages in over 100 countries)
Kein Problem mit Schwierigen Menschen (German)
Tratando con Gente Difícil (Spanish)
Traiter avec des personnes difficiles (French)
Comunicareaea cu oameni dificili (Romanian)

Dealing with Difficult Situations – at Work and at Home
Tratando con Situationes Dificiles (Spanish)

Dealing with Difficult Spouses and Children
Tratando con Cónyuges y Niños Difíciles

Dealing with Difficult Relatives and In-Laws
Tratando con parientes difíciles y en leyes

Dealing with School Bullying
Tratando con la Intimidación en la Escouela (Spanish)

Dealing with Workplace Bullying
Tratando con Intimidación en el lugar de trabajo

Keeping Our Children Safe
Mantenera Nuestros Hijos Seguros (Spanish)

Dealing with Domestic Violence and Child Abuse

Retirement Village Bullies
Just say no
What am I going to do with the rest of my life?
Interpersonal Communication at Work
Change? Not me!
Creative Problem-Solving & Decision-Making
Customer Service that Works
Teambuilding

iii

How Women can advance in business
Before Tying the Knot – Questions couples must ask each
other before they marry!
Survival Skills for Supervisors and Managers
Human Resources at its Best!
Human Resources Policies and Procedures - Australia
Employee Handbook
Easy Come – Hard to go – The Art of Hiring, Disciplining and
Firing Employees
Time and Stress – Today's silent killers
Take Command of your Future – Make things Happen!
The Presenter
Belly Laughs for All! – Volumes 1 to 8
Australian Trivia
Trivia and More – 1, 2 and 3
Australian Sports Trivia
Wisdom of the World! The happy, sad & wise things in life!
Covid-19 200 Days – Facts and Fun
Covid-19 200-400 Days – Facts and Fun
Covid 400-600 Days – Facts and Fun
Covid 600-800 Days – Facts and Fun

Covid 800-1,000 Days – Facts and Fun

Fiction

I can do it! The sky's the limit!
Twists and Turns
Treacherous Livelihoods
Life Gets Complicated
Life Goes On
Life Gets Better
That Something Special
Something Missing

ACKNOWLEDGEMENTS

My gratitude is extended to the thousands of participants of my seminars who have contributed ideas on how they handled their supervisory/management roles. Special thanks to the participants of my most popular seminar, Dealing with Difficult People, who showed by their comments that their most difficult people were more often than not - their supervisors and managers.

DEDICATION

Dedicated to those participants of my Survival Skills for Supervisors and Managers and especially those who had been given supervisory and management positions with little or no training. Many of those participants paid for their own training because their companies simply would not do so.

SURVIVAL SKILLS FOR
SUPERVISORS AND MANAGERS
Guidelines for business success

Table of Contents

- How to avoid being misunderstood
- Skill of paraphrasing
- Skill of feedback
- Process of feedback
- Feedback steps
- Non-verbal communication
- Space bubbles
- Territory
- Physical clues
- Employee's body language

- Three criteria required for problem solving
- Sample problem
- Dealing with your own problems
- Problem solving and decision-making guide
- Driving and restraining forces
- Brainstorming
- Planning for problem solving
- The importance of planning
- Planning factors
- Jobs skills inventory chart
- The change process
- Meeting objections head-on
- Making change happen
- Conflict resolution
- Creative problem solving

- Qualities of a good trainer
- Teaching adults
- Characteristics of adult learners
- Differences in adult/child learners
- Learning process

- How to 'lock in' training
- One-on-one training
- Determining training needs
- Testing abilities of employees
- Dimensions tested
- Manpower planning
- Training needs of supervisors
- Learning a new skill
- Training of others
- Retention of information
- Training vs. development
- Career development
- Training procedure
- Tangible/intangible behaviour
- Setting objectives
- Sample objectives
- Identifying costs of training
- Methods of instruction
- Methods I use
- Preparing for a seminar/workshop
- Group vs. individual activities
- Technical vs. life skills
- Theoretical vs. practical training
- Bridging
- Timing of training segments
- Use of training aids
- Re-enforcement of training
- How to keep participants motivated
- Instructor's apparel
- Presentation skills

- Conducting meetings
- Role of the chairperson
- Planning a meeting

- Using and developing group's unique talents and abilities
- Overcoming cultural or personality differences
- Evaluate
- Follow-up
- Preparing for a meeting
- Avoiding planning blunders
- The use of questions at meetings
- How to chair a meeting
- Types of meetings
- Meeting traps
- Problem participants

INTRODUCTION

When I first started offering my *Dealing with Difficult People* seminars way back in the early '80s, I assumed that the most difficult group of people faced by those in the workplace would be difficult clients. My second guess was difficult colleagues, co-workers or workmates. I was wrong in making these assumptions because overwhelmingly, the most difficult people identified by my participants were their supervisors or managers!

Why did this happen? It was because most of their supervisors/managers/department heads (and anyone else responsible for getting work done through other people) had not received the basic training necessary for them to successfully supervise others. These difficult supervisors made mistakes such as:

- Embarrass their staff by disciplining them in front of workmates or clients.

- Label staff's behaviour (stupid, dumb) or make sarcastic remarks, instead of trying to correct the actual behaviour of the staff member.

- Don't give recognition for a job well done. Instead, they concentrate on the two percent of the things their staff do incorrectly, instead of the ninety-eight percent they do properly.

- When dealing with customer complaints, they don't back up their staff and don't give employees a chance to tell their side of the story before acting. (They should say to the client, *"Let me investigate this and I'll get back to you."*

- Don't provide an up-to-date job description with key performance indicators (KPIs) and standards of performance for the tasks performed by their staff.

- Don't provide the necessary training to fill the gap between job requirements and employee's skills.
- Conduct performance appraisals on staff without a proper job description upon which to base their evaluation. (If the employee doesn't know what's expected of him/her and the supervisor doesn't know either - how can a fair evaluation of the employee's performance be conducted?)
- Have one set of company rules for staff - another for themselves. Bend the rules when clients go over the head of front-line staff, causing embarrassment for staff members.
- No set policy and procedure manuals available. Rules and regulations of the company are not clearly defined.
- Harass staff (either through bullying or sexual harassment).
- Do nothing to improve the employee's interest in their jobs. Some are afraid their employees are now ready to compete for their job, so do as little as possible to develop their skills for their next step up. (It's a proven fact that more supervisors are *not* promoted because there is nobody prepared to take over their existing job.)
- Are not available when their staff needs their help. They say they have an "open door policy," but are always "too busy" to deal with their staff's problems.
- Won't listen to their staff's suggestions about better ways to complete tasks. The person doing the job normally has the best ideas on how to do the job better, faster and more efficiently.
- Are perfectionists and expect everything to be done perfectly. Just because they can do the job in ten minutes (they have fifteen years' experience) they expect the newcomer to do it in the same amount of time with the same amount of accuracy.
- Allow nepotism to flourish in their company (hiring friends and relatives).

If this describes your actions - seriously consider getting the necessary tools to do your supervisory or management job properly.

When I became aware of how desperately supervisors/managers needed this training, I decided to expand the seminars I offered (through colleges, universities and private industries) to include one on supervisory skills. After 900 hours of research, I ended up with over one hundred pages of handouts. This was a "crash course" because most companies could not spare their staff for more than two or three days at a time.

Since then, thousands of participants worldwide have attended the seminar. Participant's evaluations ranged from, *"Where were you when I first got my supervisory job?"* to, *"I had an M.B.A. and still hadn't learned what I needed to know to be an effective supervisor. Your seminar filled that gap."*

The success of my seminar and the fact that I have already written several books already, stimulated me to put my findings into book form so I could share the information with a larger audience.

This book is geared towards those who might be entering a supervisory or management position, those who have been making the above mistakes and those who are already supervisors or managers but are running into difficulties doing their jobs properly.

CHAPTER ONE

THE ROLE OF THE

SUPERVISOR/MANAGER

Did you realise the responsibilities you took on when you agreed to take that promotion to the position of supervisor or manager? Did that position ask more from you than you had expected it to? If so, you're not alone.

Most supervisors and managers (at some time or another) ask themselves, *"What was I doing when I accepted this position? It demands from me twice as much as I thought it would. Everyone's pulling at me - my boss from above, my staff from below and my new co-workers (other supervisors/managers) from the side!"*

The secret to this transition is knowledge. Knowing what you're expected to do and how you should handle different situations are the keys to successfully supervising others. No longer are you just responsible for your own actions, but you're responsible for your staffs' as well. This is the big difference between being a worker and being a person who supervises others.

What is a Supervisor?

A supervisor is anyone who is responsible for getting work done through other people. This includes clerical supervisors, foremen/women, managers, executives and even CEOs (many CEOs have **not** had basic supervisory training). Supervision isn't easy - it's hard making the transition from being told what to do, to making decisions for others. It's also difficult to rely on others to complete assignments for which you (the supervisor/manager) are held accountable.

What does it take to be a good supervisor? I'm sure you could come up with a long list of your own. Probably some of the following would be on that list:

Qualities of a Good Supervisor/Manager

- Communicates well;
- Open to new ideas;
- Flexible and organised;
- Good time manager;
- Patient;
- Foresighted;
- Keeps employees informed;
- Dresses the part;
- Is fair and consistent;
- Approachable;
- Good motivator;
- Available;
- Open to criticism;
- Delegates well;
- Uses positive reinforcement;
- Good leader;
- Gives constructive discipline;
- Self-controlled;
- Good problem solver;
- Assertive;
- Can pace him/herself;
- Empathetic;
- Knowledgeable;
- Comfortable with power;
- Encouraging of others;
- Tactful;
- Willing to accept responsibility;
- Good role model;
- Personal life is in order.

6

If you're a supervisor, ask yourself how many of the above qualities you have. Have you determined some that you don't have? Is there anything you can do to gain those qualities?

Why do supervisors fail?

Think of supervisors you've worked for in the past. Did any of them do things that made them failure as a supervisor? In addition to NOT having the qualities (listed above) the following can also result in failure for supervisors.

These supervisors are:

- Indecisive;
- 2-faced;
- Too authoritarian;
- Too friendly;
- On a power trip;
- Supervising former peers;
- Promoted too early;
- Late;
- Procrastinators;
- Perfectionists;
- Indecisive;
- Afraid to delegate;
- Workaholics;
- Disliked by staff;
- Inconsistent;
- Distracted;
- Moody;
- Unpredictable.

These supervisors have:

- Poor work ethic;
- Poor judgement;
- Poor leadership abilities;

7

- Nervous or emotional problems.

These supervisors:

- Ignore problems;
- Show bias or favouritism;
- Lack training;
- Don't back up staff;
- Harass staff;
- Don't keep promises;
- Expect too much of others;
- Their staff more qualified than they are;
- Use passive or aggressive behaviour;
- Abuse drugs or alcohol;
- Lack team spirit;
- Family life in chaos;
- Allow nepotism (relatives or friends in company).

Do you have any of the above undesirable qualities? If so, what could you do to remove them that will make you a better supervisor?

The Role of the Supervisor/Manager:

If you're in a supervisory position now or are getting ready for one, you'll have little success in fulfilling the requirements of your role unless you have all the following responsibilities:

1. Delegate work to subordinates.
2. Check subordinate's work.

Most supervisors and foremen have these two responsibilities, but unfortunately some don't have the next two:

3. Conduct performance appraisals.
4. Discipline subordinates.

Another responsibility that's an advantage is:

5. Hire your own staff.

If you have only the first two responsibilities, you're in a "lead hand" position. This is a "no win" situation, so you should speak to the person who conducts performance appraisals and/or gives the discipline. Suggest that they handle the first two responsibilities as well or that you have the latter two (three if possible) so you can do your job effectively.

To give you more information on these essential responsibilities:

Delegate Work to subordinates: These are the actual tasks you give to your subordinates for completion.

Check subordinate's work: This is where you check your employee's completion of tasks to see that they're done properly. You'll check quantity and quality of the task performed and how long it took to complete.

Conduct performance appraisals: YOU should be the one that does the performance appraisal for all your subordinates; nobody else. Your manager shouldn't do them, because s/he's not directly responsible for the work of your subordinates. S/he might review your findings to see if they're fair, but YOU complete the appraisal on each employee you supervise.

Discipline subordinates: Because your staff ends up making you look either good or bad, you need this control to correct production and/or behaviour problems. Most companies withhold permission for supervisors to fire employees due to the importance of fending off charges of "wrongful dismissal." This should be handled by those specially trained in its implementation. (This and the next topic are covered in my next book: *Easy Come - Hard to Go - The Art of Hiring and Firing Employees*).

Hire your own staff: This is a plus - but not always allowed by companies. Try your best to have input into the hiring of the people who work for you. If you're on different wavelengths, it can be very difficult for both of you to work as a team.

How does your supervisory position measure up? If you don't have the first four responsibilities, you're in trouble. You'll receive questionable respect from your subordinates and have little control over the outcome of their work. If you don't have that control over your employees and they do an unsatisfactory job - who looks bad? You do!

The Person in the Middle:

Many supervisors didn't prepare for the transition from worker to supervisor. They were not aware of how they'd be "The person in the middle." Try to visualise the supervisor as being in the centre of a five-petalled star. This person is no longer just responsible for his/her own actions, but responsible to the following groups. They're:

1. Subordinate to their bosses (usually managers).
2. Responsible to other staff groups in the implementation of policies and procedures.
3. If they work with a unionised company, they're responsible to unions as mediators.
4. Responsible for their own staff.
5. Responsible for co-operating with other supervisors.

Here are more details on these responsibilities:

A. Responsibility to the department or company

1. Knowledge of supervisory techniques and the skill to use them.
2. Production - quality and quantity of work.
3. Good leadership and handling of employee relations.
4. Economy in operation and cost effectiveness.
5. Planning and co-coordinating work with other sections to avoid duplication of costs and effort.
6. Knowledge of and continued improvement of policies and procedures as required.

7. Establishment of standards of performance for one's work group - both quantitative and qualitative.
8. Estimates of budgets and control of costs within estimates.
9. Proper care and use of equipment, materials and supplies.
10. Loyalty and open communication to one's own supervisor.
11. Knowledgeable about company organisational charts and where his/her unit fits into the overall picture.

Responsibility to Staff:

1. Indoctrination and introduction of new employees. You introduce new employee to other staff. Delegate one employee to show your new employee the "ropes." This would enable the new employee to learn such things as; where to find the washroom, when and where coffee breaks and lunch breaks are held, etc.
2. Knowledge of rules and regulations. Have you read your company's policy and procedures manuals - if not, why not? They contain the rules, regulations, policies and procedures that relate to all employees. Are these policies and procedures up-to-date? If not, see that they're updated so you and your staff know what the company expects of you.
3. Adequate instruction so employees can complete assignments properly. (See Chapter 8 -Training and Development).
4. Delegation of accurate, definite and reasonable assignments.
5. Recognition, respect and praise when due.
6. Fair evaluation of performance and treatment.
7. Good working conditions and pleasant work group.
8. Having a good disposition, appearance, and attitude.
9. Freedom to get on with the job without too much interference.
10. Staff allowed freedom of expression and given constructive criticism.
11. Keep staff informed of all changes and reasons for them.

12. Sympathetic help and consideration with personal problems.
13. Loyalty and the defence of the group. Be willing to stand up for your staff.

Responsibility to Unions:

What does the union expect of the supervisor?

1. That you'll give fair treatment to all employees.
2. Avoid grievances by using good management practices.
3. Communication of all changes affecting employee relations.
4. A reasonable approach in formal discussions.

D. Responsibility to Other Supervisors:

What do supervisors expect from each other?

1. Co-operation and a mutual understanding.
2. Knowledgeable of objectives, responsibilities and priorities of the company and departments.
3. A reasonable approach to conflicting interests.
4. Knowledge that if anything is changed in one department, it may affect other departments.

Overall Responsibilities:

These responsibilities fall under the heading of five management functions:

Planning: coordinating, scheduling, budgeting and setting production objectives;

Organising: task identification, giving of responsibility and authority;

Staffing: job requirements, recruitment and selection, training and development;

Directing: guiding, supervising, motivating and orienting;

Controlling: performance appraisals, disciplining, assessing objectives and correcting errors.

The role of the supervisor then, is to get work done through other people by planning organising, staffing, directing, and controlling.

Here are some other supervisory terms used when delegating tasks:

Responsibility:

This is the actual task that requires completion.

Authority:

Means the subordinate has the authority to complete the task. For example: You've given one of your staff the responsibility of ordering office supplies for your department. The employee makes a list of what staff members require and takes that list to the Supply Depot. The Supply Clerk refuses to fill the order and says, *"You don't have signing authority for your department."*

You made a mistake - caused embarrassment to your employee - and wasted valuable time.

Another supervisor asked one of his staff to go to the Human Resources Department to pick up an employee's personnel file. Because the file was confidential, the employee required written permission to release it. The employee returned without the file.

So, make sure your staff has not only the responsibility (the task) but also the authority to fulfil their obligations.

Many supervisors believe that if they delegate a task to an employee, they can divorce themselves from the responsibility of that task. This is not so. The following information will help you understand this concept:

13

Accountability:

There are two levels of accountability:

1. Delegated Accountability:

The supervisor gives the responsibility (task) to the employee. The employee is accountable to the supervisor for the task.

2. Final Accountability:

The final accountability remains with the supervisor who delegated the task to the employee. Because you have this final accountability, your staff has the ability to make you look good or bad. This is why it's essential for you to have the authority to discipline staff and conduct performance appraisals.

The role of the worker vs. the supervisor:

Here are the major differences between workers and supervisors:

- Supervisor: Typically works with people, ideas and plans.
  Worker: Typically works with tools, material and equipment.
- Supervisor: Produces through others by training them and by building a climate that encourages them to perform well.
  Worker: Directly produces a product or performs a service.
- Supervisor: Often must make decisions concerning employees, material, machines, and schedules with incomplete information.
  Worker: Often works under precise instructions on specific jobs.
- Supervisor: Plans work with and for others.
  Worker: Follows plans for own job.
- Supervisor: Responsible for work of others
  Worker: Responsible for own job.
- Supervisor: More duties in varied areas.
  Worker: Duties usually limited and competitive.

- Supervisor: Essential part of the organisation.
- Worker: Essential part of an organisation.

My role as a supervisor:

What is your role as a supervisor? In writing (being as realistic as possible) complete the following questions:

1. My duties as a supervisor:
2. Supervisory duties I feel I do well:
3. Supervisory duties I must handle better:
4. What specific training do I need?

Did you have trouble completing #1? This would happen if you didn't have an accurate up-to-date position description. If you don't have one, see Chapter 3 to help you prepare an accurate one.

#2 will identify things you are good at. (You should do things you're good at as often as possible). If your job doesn't give you this satisfaction, obtain training or move on to a more suitable position.

If you've identified anything in #3, decide whether you need clarification from your manager or require on-the-job or outside training.

In #4, if you need training, by all means ask for it. Because of belt-tightening, many companies may tell you they can't offer you the training you think you require. Try negotiating with them. Offer to pay half of the costs of training or sign an agreement that if you leave the company within two years you'll pay for the training.

If they still refuse to pay for your training - pay for it yourself! It will be one of the best investments you can make and will put you ahead of others in your company who didn't receive the training.

Stop waiting for "big brother" (your company) or something external to change your life. Somehow find a way to get the training you need.

Supervising Former Peers:

In talking with supervisors (especially new ones) they identified that criticising or disciplining employees is their hardest supervisory responsibility. This is especially true if they're supervising former peers.

How should you handle the first day on the job where you're suddenly responsible for supervising your former peers (who also applied for your position?) What kinds of problems could this cause? What kinds of feelings are involved? How will the unsuccessful co-workers react to you being their new supervisor?

Former Peers may:

- Feel jealous, envious, angry;
- Feel they are better qualified;
- Unco-operative;
- Sabotage your efforts;
- Won't respect you as a leader;
- Gang up on you;
- Expect favouritism or bias on your part;
- They know your weaknesses and might take advantage of them.

New Supervisor may:

- Go on an ego trip;
- May feel alienated;
- In over his/her head;
- May show bias, favouritism.

Let's say you're the new supervisor and you know that several of your former co-workers applied for the position you obtained. You'll likely fail if you don't handle that first day or week properly. It's necessary to diffuse any feelings of envy and jealousy your new subordinates might have. Hopefully, before your first day on the job, your manager will have explained to your former co-workers why they did not receive the promotion. This should not be your job, so don't try to handle it.

On your first day, your manager should call a meeting where s/he introduces you to your new staff. The manager then leaves, so you can take over the meeting. How you conduct the rest of the meeting often determines how your new staff accepts you.

If you anticipate hard feelings, deal with your former co-workers' feelings first. Start by saying, *"I know a few of you applied for and wanted this promotion. I can understand that you may feel a little upset that I got the position instead of you. The company chose me, so what we do from now on depends on how all of us work together. I need your support to handle my job properly. In return, I'll do everything I can to be a good supervisor. Can I count on you to help me do a good job?"*

Then have each member make a commitment to you that they will give you their support. Ask, *"Margie, how about you? Can I count on your support?" "Dave?"* And cover every employee that reports to you. The body language of the employee will tell you whether to expect further difficulty from any employee. If s/he has made a verbal commitment to you, s/he's much more likely to cooperate in the future.

If, however, you see reluctance in his/her answer, don't let the moment pass by. State, *"Margie, I detect a little hesitancy from you? What can I do to make the situation a little easier for you?"* If the employee remains difficult, you may have to talk to her privately to deal with the issue. If poor productivity or negative behaviour continues (and especially if it's sabotage)

17

activate stronger discipline. Nip the problem in the bud - don't let it grow and flourish and contaminate others in your section.

You should also state that you will be having meetings with each person reporting to you. Say, *"Even though I have worked with all of you, I don't really know what your roles are. Within the next few weeks, I will examine your job descriptions and personnel files so I can discuss your career plans and any issues you have with how you do your job."*

Socialising with your new staff:

Before your promotion, you normally went out on Friday night after work with a few of your co-workers. Should you still socialise after work now that you're supervising your former co-workers? Many would say yes - that if you didn't, your staff would assume that the position *"had gone to your head,"* or, *"you're too good for them now!"*

Be careful on this one. If you do still socialise with your former co-workers, follow one rule. That rule is that you never talk about business during social times. This is necessary, especially if you do not socialise with all your new staff. It's easy for other staff to assume you'll show favouritism to the ones you're socialising with.

It's time too, to look at your new situation. You now have a new peer group. What is this new peer group? They're your new co-workers - other supervisors. Cultivate their friendship so you can obtain information through the informal network that keeps you knowledgeable about what is going on in your company.

We'll now move on to the different leadership styles you can use with your new staff.

CHAPTER TWO

LEADERSHIP STYLES

Leadership:

John F. Kennedy believed leadership to be *"Inspiring people to put forth their best effort."*

General Eisenhower demonstrated leadership with a simple piece of string. He'd pull it on a table and say: *"Pull it and it will follow wherever you wish - push it and it will go nowhere at all."*

It's just that way when it comes to leading people. Leadership isn't something that comes automatically just because you have people working for you. Leadership depends on followers. If people won't follow a boss's lead voluntarily - if they always have to be forced - s/he's not a good leader.

Leadership depends on your ability to make people want to follow, voluntarily. Bosses who prod (rather than lead) rarely get the best out of those who work for them. All these employees want is to keep their boss off their backs.

Most people want to do a good job, as long as someone appreciates their efforts and encourages them. That's where a leader must put his or her greatest effort - in showing employees that their work is valued and appreciated. Keep in touch with what and how your subordinates are doing. Supervisors must get away from their desks and spend time in the work area so they "get a feel" for the actual working conditions.

Keep an "open door" policy so employees having problems fulfilling their tasks can discuss alternative approaches.

Keep employees informed of any changes that have occurred which will affect the outcome of their duties.

Leadership Skills and Traits:

Here are some of the skills and traits of a good leader:

- Respected by peers;
- Energetic;
- Others seek his/her ideas;
- Enthusiastic;
- Is a risk-taker;
- Influential;
- Persevering;
- Independent;
- Comfortable with power;
- Goal oriented;
- Knows what's going on;
- Self-confident, assertive;
- Has many new ideas;
- Creative;
- Organised;
- Flexible;
- Caring of others;
- Empathetic;
- Willing listener;
- Understanding;
- Good motivator;
- Personal life in order;
- Delegates well;
- Sense of humour;
- Trainer;
- Responsible.

How many of these do you have? Are you missing any? What do you think you can do to improve those you feel you're missing?

Use of Leadership Skills

In addition to the above-mentioned skills, add the following supervisory skills:

Intellectual/Cognitive skills

1. Figures out what's wrong; shows others how to solve problems.
2. Handles abstract ideas and sees a broad perspective; sees the whole picture, while others may focus on parts.
3. Plans and follows through.
4. Projects into the future, seeing consequences of decisions.

Personal skills:

1. Judges appropriateness of own decisions, directions or suggestions; gauges appropriateness of own timing in these same areas.
2. Copes with unpleasantness. (This would include disciplining or laying-off employees or helping employee deal with personal or co-worker problems).
3. Is able to absorb interpersonal stress.
4. Is able to tolerate ambiguity, delay and frustration.

Interpersonal skills:

1. Listens to, observes and recognises the skills and abilities of others.
2. Interacts with others easily; has the ability to inspire confidence in others.
3. Perceives and articulates unstated feelings; recognises and states goals, problems, ideas and interests of group.
4. Follows well. Does not bad-mouth his/her superiors.
5. Supports members of the group; accepts responsibility; is able to determine appropriate behaviours and courses of action.

21

6. Organises others, directs activities, delegates responsibility and establishes the mood of the group.

Good Leadership:

Good leadership is a precious commodity. Many employees have a difficult time identifying someone who was a good leader.

Can you remember a supervisor in your past who brought out the best in you? What did s/he do that was different from the average leader?

These exceptional supervisors probably gave the impression that:

a) S/he had faith in his/her staff's abilities.
b) Took the time to find out what his/her employee's abilities really were;
c) Knew which employee was a whiz at organising a large quantity of material and let them use that talent;
d) Knew which employee had the talents to deal with a particularly difficult client.

To accumulate this knowledge, wise supervisors:

a) Know the talents and abilities of their staff;
b) Have examined employee personnel files to learn what their staff have done in the past, which organisations they may belong to etc.;
c) Have enough interest in his/her staff as human beings to identify their strengths (and weaknesses) and to use their strengths in the workplace. (See chapter 3: delegation).

S/he trained you properly and:

a) Coached or trained employees properly before setting them free to do their jobs;

b) Gave his/her staff enough rope to do their job, but pulled them in when it looked as if they were heading for trouble;

c) Made sure that the gap was filled between the employee's qualifications and the needs of the position by either on-the-job or outside training; and

d) Tried to make sure his/her employees were ready for their next promotion. (See chapter 8, training and development).

S/he encouraged staff:

a) By concentrating on the 98% of the work his/her staff did right, not the 2% of the work they did wrong;

b) Made sure his/her staff was aware of their responsibilities;

c) Made sure his/her employees knew that it was okay to make mistakes, as long as they learned from them and didn't make them again. (See chapter 4 - Motivation).

S/he recognised his/her employees' talents:

a) Showed them talents they didn't even know they had;

b) Encouraged them to stretch their talents and abilities;

c) Helped employees reach their full potential;

d) Made employees feel like doing almost anything for them, if they asked;

e) Found their employee's "hot buttons" that made them want to do their best for him/her; and

f) Seemed to know what motivated each member of his/her staff. (See chapter 4 - Motivation).

Bad Leadership:

Can you remember a supervisor in your past who brought out the worst in you? What did they do that made this happen? Did they give you the impression that:

1. You couldn't do anything right. Did they concentrate only on what you did wrong, but never said a word about what

23

you did right? Did they give you the impression that you weren't very smart?

2. That you needed a firm hand to make you work hard. Did they use an authoritarian (19th century) style of management with you? Were they important, but you weren't?

3. That you didn't need to know anything about the company except how to do your job correctly? Did they imply that the less you knew about the company, the better it would be? Did they appear unsure of their own abilities?

4. Never considered you for a promotion. Did they keep you from obtaining the training you required to progress in the company? Were they threatened by your talents and abilities; react as if you knew too much?

These are all characteristics of a supervisor who sets you up for failure. Make sure you make every effort to be like the first kind of supervisor described - the supervisor you respected.

Do you feel leaders are born - or do they develop as they mature? Both situations are true. If you've ever watched a group of very young children together, you'll soon see one or more leaders emerge. Others will be contented to follow these leaders.

Later, when these children grew up, they could either remain the same or change course completely. Some early leaders become the "class clown" who often alienate others and have their leadership taken from them. Some early "followers," after consistent positive feedback from their parents, teachers and friends, become self-assured enough to become leaders. Many become leaders when they gained the knowledge, maturity and self-confidence required.

Leadership Styles:

Leadership styles differ from highly authoritarian (Theory X) to highly employee participative (Theory Y). Most leadership

24

styles have changed from authoritarian to participative in the last century because:

Changing social values. The class system of the 19th century meant there were large social and business gaps between management and workers. It was seldom possible for a worker to obtain a managerial position unless something unusual happened.

Legislation protecting workers' rights. No longer are 10-year-olds expected to put in 16-hour days. Employees have regular coffee and lunch breaks. Employees now have vacation and statutory holidays, etc.

Supply and demand on the labour market. Mass production of items and diversification of products has meant there are more jobs with more qualifications required, which lessens the gap between workers and management.

Competition - both domestic and foreign. The availability of communication and travel between countries has made it possible for international trade. This increased competition within countries as well.

Declining profit margins. In the early 1900s, it was not unheard of to obtain 30% profit for a product or service because there were few middlemen. Now there are many middlemen involved, rather than the producer selling directly to the consumer.

Profit margins are lower because of mass-production of articles through the availability of automation and robotics. Competition with international markets has caused profit margins to remain low.

Higher level of formal education of workers and management. The gap between workers and management has lessened because there are more intermediary levels between the two extremes. Most free world populations believe that anyone can achieve the level of position they want, if they want it badly enough. They believe the opportunity is available for anyone to become what they want in life providing they have the ability to do so.

Unions and their power. Unions stepped in at the beginning of the last century to fight for the rights of the workers. They were necessary to take employees out of the squalor they often had to work in. On the negative side, unions today are making it almost impossible for some companies to stay in business. This in turn, increases the unemployment level.

What is Your Leadership Style?

Here are the differences between the two following theories:

Theory Y vs Theory X:

Theory Y Assumption 1: People are naturally active; they set goals and enjoy striving.
Theory X Assumptions: People are naturally lazy. They prefer to do nothing.

Theory Y Assumption 2: People seek many satisfactions in work, pride in achievement, enjoyment of process, sense of contribution, pleasure in association and new challenges.
Theory X Assumptions: People work mostly for money, status and rewards.

Theory Y Assumption 3: The main force keeping people productive in their work is the desire to achieve their personal and social goals.
Theory X Assumptions: The main force keeping people productive in their work is fear of being demoted or fired.

Theory Y Assumption 4: People normally mature beyond childhood. They aspire to independence, self-fulfilment and responsibility.
Theory X Assumptions: People remain children grown larger – they're naturally dependent on leaders.

Theory Y Assumption 5: People close to the situation see and feel what is needed and are capable of self-direction.
Theory X Assumptions: People expect and depend on direction from above. Don't want to think for themselves.

Theory Y Assumption 6: People who understand and care about what they're doing can devise and improve their own methods of doing work.
Theory X Assumptions: People need to be told, shown and trained in proper methods of work.

Theory Y Assumption 7: People need a sense that they're respected as capable of assuming responsibility and self-direction.
Theory X Assumptions: People need supervisors who will watch them closely enough to be able to praise good work and correct errors.

Theory Y Assumption 8: People seek to give meaning to their lives by identifying with nations, communities, churches, unions, companies and causes.
Theory X Assumptions: People have little concern beyond their immediate material interests.

Theory Y Assumption 9: People need ever-increasing understanding. They need to know why they're doing what they're doing and how it fits in with the company's objectives.
Theory X Assumptions: People need specific instruction on what to do and how to do it. Larger policy issues are none of their business.

Theory Y Assumption 10: People crave genuine respect from their fellow man.
Theory X Assumptions: Pay people well and they'll be happy.

Theory Y Assumption 11: People are naturally integrated. When work and play are too sharply separated, both deteriorate.

Theory X Assumptions: People are naturally compartmentalised. Work demands are entirely different from leisure activities.

Theory Y Assumption 12: People naturally tire of monotonous routine and enjoy new experiences. To some degree, everyone is creative.
Theory X Assumptions: People naturally resist change. They prefer to stay in the old ruts.

Do you find you have to use Theory X on certain employees? For instance, consider #6. Let's say you need to delegate an identical task to two employees. Some employees become very upset if you tell them exactly what steps they're to take to complete an assignment. They're accustomed to receiving assignments and completing them in their own way. They crave variety and new ways of completing tasks.

Other employees are very upset if you don't give them explicit instructions and explain every little detail to them. They're often the same employees who panic if you want them to do something a different way than the way they've done it in the past.

Did you agree with #10 under Theory X assumptions? Do you believe that if you *"Pay people well, they'll be happy?"* For some employees this is true, but the vast majority of employees can be stimulated to give good performance for a myriad of other reasons (see Chapter 4 - Motivation).

Did you agree with #11, Theory Y Assumptions? If you look at your friends and acquaintances, you'll find that if they truly enjoy their work, they'll probably do something complementary in their time off. For instance, auto mechanics may spend some of their leisure time looking after their friends' cars. Hairdressers may do their friends' hair and lecturers may offer their services free to non-profit organisations.

Getting to Know Your Staff:

Do you really know your staff? Do you know what makes them want to do a good job for you? Are you aware of their past employment and what they do with their leisure time? If you don't, you're probably wasting many of their talents and abilities or are delegating tasks to the wrong employee. To find out how you are in this department, complete the following questions:

Test yourself:

How much effort have you taken to do the following using the following scale:

Very Good   Okay   Not Good

1. Get acquainted with each subordinate?
2. Review personnel files?
3. Discover and allay fears of employees?
4. Obtain current job descriptions and position objectives for each position?
5. Can others take over when you're not there?
6. Spend time listening to people and encouraging expression of their views?
7. Obtain agreement on job standards?
8. Find out what people like and dislike?
9. Develop team working commitments?
10. Demonstrate your real interest in your subordinates?
11. Keep open-door policy?
12. Discipline effectively?
13. Motivate effectively?
14. Use time effectively?
15. Plan and schedule effectively?
16. Train effectively?

If you've identified any *not good* areas, the following might help you correct them.

- Get acquainted with each subordinate. It's surprising how little some supervisors know about the people who work for them. They fail to recognise that their staff (more often than not) have hidden talents that they could be using to their company's advantage. Unfortunately, most don't care enough to really get to know their staff:
- Review Personnel files. What information is on an employee's file that can be useful to you?

Their application form or resume can tell you a lot. These could give you valuable information relating to their level of responsibility in past positions, where their talents lie and other areas of expertise. The information that they're the president of their community club might identify that they have administrative abilities you may not be aware of.

Employment interview notes. Be careful there are no discriminatory comments on this sheet.

Job description (you may find that it is outdated or inaccurate which should trigger you to update it).

Performance appraisals (both positive information as well as negative).

Disciplinary warnings (may identify troublesome employees).

Health care and pension information.

Can an employee ask to see his/her personnel file? Yes, they can. You must make it available to them within 24 hours of a written request to see it. Because of this, you should make sure there is nothing on the employee's personnel file that the employee doesn't know about. Remove any discriminatory comments that may have been made on interview notes. Most supervisors have a secondary file they keep locked in their desks somewhere. This confidential file keeps such things as notes relating to both positive and negative issues. Negative comments may include: times an employee has been late, absences or other behavioural or production problems.

Discover and allay fears of employees.

If your employees are afraid there may be a lay-off (and you know otherwise) - keep them informed. Many employees are afraid of automation - believe they can't keep up.

If you're going to install a new computer, make sure employees know that they will have ample time and training to learn the new system. Or they may be afraid of being replaced by a more technically knowledgeable person.

Obtain current job descriptions and position objectives for each employee.

How can you evaluate the performance of your employees, if neither of you knows what they are to do? Accurate, up-to-date job descriptions are essential for the sooth running of any business.

Obtain agreement on job standards.

Each task in a job description should have clearly defined job standards so the supervisor can evaluate how well the employee's doing.

Can others take over when you're not there?

If you haven't prepared someone to take over, then you haven't been delegating properly.

Spend time listening to people and encouraging expression of their views.

If more supervisors listened to the suggestions of their staff, things would probably progress much faster. Usually, the person performing the task has a more realistic idea on how tasks should be performed faster and easier. It's worth a

31

supervisor's time to listen to their staff's suggestions. If you can't use his/her ideas, make sure s/he knows why.

Find out what people like and dislike about their jobs. This is something that most supervisors don't question. When supervisors know the likes and dislikes of their staff, they can delegate better and watch for lapses in productivity.

Develop team working commitments. When work requires employees to work harmoniously together, getting everyone pulling in unison can be one of a supervisor's major tasks. Each group has their problem members, and a supervisor must be wary of these members and take corrective action.

Demonstrate your real interest in your subordinates. It's surprising how much this can do to help relationships between bosses and employees. A simple, *"I understand congratulations are in order! I just heard about the three goals your son scored for his soccer team that allowed them to win the tournament!"*

Keep open-door policy. This doesn't just mean that your door is open - it means that you're available and willing to help your staff when they come to you for help. Remember that's one of your major tasks - getting things done through other people and to guide them through problem areas.

Discipline effectively. You may end up with more problems than you started with unless you conduct disciplinary interviews correctly. Your goal should be to bring out the best in your staff – not their worst.

Motivate effectively. Motivating individuals can be a major challenge: it's up to you to find employees' "Hot Buttons."

Use time effectively. Not only are you responsible for using your time effectively, but you're responsible for properly using the time of your subordinates as well. This makes time management one of a supervisor's prime pre-requisites.

Effective time management reduces the stress level of all involved.

Plan and schedule effectively. Explained above.

Train effectively. Most companies have had to pull in their belts relating to training their staff, but it remains a company's most valuable investment. Because in-house training is so much more cost-effective, supervisors who have the ability to train their staff are definite assets to their companies.

Leadership Behaviour:

If someone were to ask you what leadership style you use, what would you answer? Are you like most people and use a variety of styles depending on the situation and the particular employee you're guiding? Supervisors should use the leadership style warranted to meet individual circumstances. Here are seven different styles of management that range from boss-centred (authoritarian) to employee-centred management:

Try to think of times where you've used these leadership styles:

1. **Supervisor makes the decision and announces it:** This is definitely a Theory X style of management. In this case, the boss identifies a problem, considers alternative solutions, chooses one of them and then reports this decision to the subordinates for implementation. They may or may not have considered what their subordinates will think or feel about the decision.

   In any case, they provide little opportunity for them to participate directly in the decision-making process. Coercion is or isn't used or implied. An example of where this leadership style could be used is when a rule or regulation must be enforced and implemented.

For example: *"From now on, customer complaints are given directly to Joe Smith."*

2. **Supervisor "sells" their decision**: As before, supervisors take responsibility for identifying the problem and deciding what to do. However, rather than simply announcing their decision they take the additional step of persuading their subordinates to accept it. In doing so, they recognise the possibility of some resistance among those who are faced with the decision. They seek to reduce this resistance by showing what employees have to gain from their decision.

    For example: *"We seem to be having more than our usual share of customer complaints. To spare you from having to handle them in the future, customer complaints go directly to Joe Smith."*

3. **Supervisor presents ideas and invites questions:** Here the boss has made a decision and seeks acceptance of his/her subordinates by giving a fuller explanation of the situation. After presenting the information, the supervisor invites questions so associates can better understand what s/he's trying to accomplish. This "give and take" also enables the supervisors and subordinates to explore more fully, the implications of the decision.

    For example: *"We seem to be having more than our usual share of customer complaints. To spare you from having to handle them in the future, customer complaints go directly to Joe Smith. Are there any questions?"*

4. **Supervisor presents a tentative decision subject to change:** This kind of behaviour permits the subordinates to exert some influence on the decision. The initiative for identifying and diagnosing the problem remains with the boss. Before meeting with his/her staff, the supervisor has thought the problem through and has made a tentative

decision. Before finishing it, the supervisor presents the proposed solution for the reaction of those it will affect.

The supervisor implies, *"I'd like to hear what you have to say about this plan I've developed. I appreciate your frank reactions and after our discussions, I'll decide. We seem to be having more than our usual share of customer complaints. To spare you from having to handle them in the future, I'm considering having customer complaints sent directly to Joe Smith. How do you feel about this?"*

5. **Supervisor presents the problem, gets suggestions and then makes the decision:** Up to this point, the boss has come before the group with a solution. This is not so in this case. The subordinates now get the first chance to suggest solutions. The supervisor's initial role involves identifying the problem. The function of the group becomes one of increasing the supervisor's range of possible solutions to the problem. The purpose is to capitalise on the knowledge and experience of those who are on the "firing line." From the expanded list of alternatives developed by the supervisor and the staff, the supervisor then selects the solution regarded as the most promising.

   For example: *"We seem to be having more than our usual share of customer complaints. I'm open to suggestions on how you think we can solve this problem and who should handle customer complaints in the future."* The group would then brainstorm until they came up with viable solutions.

   I've watched supervisors take three days to come up with a solution when brainstorming with the affected staff could have come up with a solution in fifteen minutes. It's a tool that far too few supervisors use. We'll be discussing brainstorming in Chapter 7.

6. **Supervisor defines the limits and requests the group to make a decision**: At this point, the supervisor passes to

the group (possibly including themselves as a member) the right to make decisions. Before doing so however, they define the problem and the boundaries within which the decision is made. An example might be the handling of a parking problem at the plant. The boss decides that this is something that involves the staff directly, so they should be directly involved in its solution.

He may tell them: *"There's an open field just north of the main plant we've decided will be used for additional employee parking. We can build underground or surface multi-level facilities, as long as the cost doesn't exceed $250,000. Within those limits, we're free to work out whatever solution makes sense to us. After we decide on a specific plan, the company will spend the available money on whatever we decide."*

7. **Supervisor permits the group to make decisions within prescribed limits**: This represents an extreme degree of group freedom, only occasionally found in formal organisations (for instance research groups). Here, the team of supervisors undertakes the identification and diagnosis of the problem, develops alternative procedures to solve it and decides on one or more of these alternative solutions. The only limits directly imposed on the group by the organisation are those specified by the superior of the team's boss. If they participate in the decision-making process, they attempt to do so with no more authority than any other member of the group. They commit themselves in advance to assist in implementing whatever decision the group makes.

    For example: Engineering firms often use this method where several peer groups work towards completion of a project. One engineer may be unofficially in charge of one project - while s/he is a subordinate or team member in another.

36

When I was Human Resources Manager for a company, I used this method. I was designated as project leader when my company wanted to produce an orientation package for new employees. At the meeting, all the department heads worked together to accomplish that goal. In another session, the Production Manager called a meeting to discuss the feasibility of hiring a third shift to cover a particularly large contract. In this case the Production Manager was the project leader.

Alternative Leadership Approaches:

Leadership is not an exact science. Decide which alternative to these leadership approaches you would choose.

1. Your subordinates are not responding lately to your friendly conversation and concern for their welfare. Their performance is in a tailspin.

   a. Encourage the use of uniform procedures and the necessity for task accomplishment.
   b. Make yourself available for discussion - but don't push.
   c. Talk with subordinates and then set goals.
   d. Intentionally do not intervene.

2. The observable performance of your group is increasing. You've been making sure that all members are aware of their roles and standards.

   a. Engage in friendly interaction but continue to make sure that all members are aware of their roles and standards.
   b. Take no definite action.
   c. Do what you can to make the group feel important and involved.
   d. Emphasise the importance of deadlines and tasks.

3. Members of your group are unable to solve a problem themselves. You have normally left them alone. Group performance and interpersonal relations have been good.

   a. Involve the group and together engage in problem solving.
   b. Let the group work it out.
   c. Act quickly and firmly to correct and redirect.
   d. Encourage group to work on problem and be available for discussion.

4. You are considering a major change. Your subordinates have a fine record of accomplishment. They respect the need for change.

   a. Allow group to have involvement in developing change - but don't push.
   b. Announce changes and then implement with close supervision.
   c. Allow group to formulate its own direction.
   d. Incorporate group recommendations, but you direct the change.

5. The performance of your group has been dropping during the last few months. Members have been unconcerned with meeting objectives. Redefining roles has helped in the past. They have continually needed to be reminded to have their tasks done on time.

   a. Allow group to formulate its own direction.
   b. Incorporate group recommendations but see that they meet objectives.
   c. Re-define goals and supervise carefully.
   d. Allow group involvement in setting goals, but don't push.

6. You stepped into an efficiently run situation. The previous administrator ran a tight ship. You want to maintain a productive situation but would like to begin humanising the environment.

   a. Do what you can to make group feel important and involved.
   b. Emphasise the importance of deadlines and tasks.

    c. Intentionally do not intervene.

    d. Get group involved in decision-making but see that they meet objectives.

7.   You are considering major changes in your organisational structure. Members of the group have made suggestions about needed change. The group has demonstrated flexibility in its day-to-day operations.

    a. Clarify the change required and supervise carefully.

    b. Gain group's approval on the change and allow members to organise the implementation.

    c. Be willing to make changes as recommended but maintain control of implementation.

    d. Avoid confrontation: leave things alone.

8.   Group performance and interpersonal relations are good. You feel somewhat unsure about your lack of direction of the group.

    a. Leave the group alone.

    b. Discuss the situation with the group and then start necessary changes.

    c. Take steps to direct subordinates toward working in a well-defined manner.

    d. Be careful of hurting boss-subordinate relations by being too forceful.

9.   Your superior has appointed you to head a task force that is far overdue in making requested recommendations for change. The group is not clear on its goals. Attendance at sessions has been poor. Their meetings have turned into social gatherings. Potentially they have the talent necessary to help, but they aren't using it.

    a. Let the group work it out.

    b. Incorporate group recommendations, but see they meet objectives.

    c. Redefine goals and supervise carefully.

    d. Allow group involvement in setting goals, but don't push.

10. Your subordinates, usually able to take responsibility, are not responding to your recent redefining of standards.

    a. Allow group involvement in redefining standards, but don't push.

    b. Redefine standards and supervise carefully.

    c. Avoid confrontation by not applying pressure.

    d. Incorporate group recommendations, but see they meet new standards.

11. You've been promoted to a new position. The previous supervisor was uninvolved in the affairs of the group. The group has adequately handled tasks and direction. Group inter-relations are good.

    a. Take steps to direct subordinates toward working in a well-defined manner.

    b. Involve subordinates in decision-making and reinforce good contribution.

    c. Discuss past performance with group and then examine the need for new practices.

    d. Continue to leave the group alone.

12. Recent information shows some internal difficulties among subordinates. The group has a remarkable record of accomplishment. Members have effectively maintained long range goals. They've worked in harmony for the past year and have the necessary qualifications to complete the task.

    a. Try out your solution with subordinates and examine the need for new practices.

    b. Allow group members to work it out themselves.

    c. Act quickly and firmly to correct and redirect.

    d. Make yourself available for discussion but be careful of hurting boss-subordinate relations.

The correct answers are:

1. Staff needs leadership, so: a or c
2. No real problems here, so: b or c
3. Staff needs leadership, so: a or c
4. Low-key leadership required here, so: a or d
5. Staff needs leadership, so: b or c
6. No real problems here, so: a or d
7. Staff needs leadership, so: b or c
8. No real problems here, so: a or d
9. Staff needs leadership, so: c
10. Problems with your leadership style, so: d
11. No real problems here, so: b or c
12. Staff needs leadership, so: c or d

As you can see, leadership styles differ depending on the situation and the person being lead. Now that you understand about leadership, you'll need to learn how to delegate downward to your staff so that the best qualified person, at the lowest possible cost, completes each task.

CHAPTER THREE

DELEGATION

When a job becomes too complex, too diverse or too large for one person to handle, the need for more employees and for delegation arises.

Delegation:

Delegation means a supervisor has given a subordinate the responsibility and authority to get the job done. The employee is accountable to the supervisor for successful completion of the task. The supervisor in turn, has the final accountability for the work being completed correctly. Therefore, the employee either makes the supervisor look good or look bad depending on how well they complete their tasks.

Excuses for Non-Delegation:

Many supervisors give the excuses:

- *"It must be done right now. By the time I give it to someone else, explain what I want them to do and check to make sure it's done right - I could have finished it and three more jobs besides!"*
- *"This job is SO important that only I can do it."*
- *"I'm afraid my staff will fail."*
- *"I LIKE doing this job myself."*
- *"I can do this better than anyone else."*
- *"If I delegate to others - what will I do?"*
- *"I don't want my people to think I'm a tyrant."*

Once the employee is properly trained, does the job and knows what you expect, s/he will be able to handle these assignments. This allows you to concentrate your efforts on more important issues.

43

Risks of Delegation:

Why don't some supervisors delegate enough tasks to subordinates?

1. Loss of control. They'll have to take the chance that the subordinate may goof-up.
2. They'll lose their own job. Some supervisors feel that if they delegate everything, they'll have no job left to do.
3. Heaven forbid - suppose the employee becomes better than they are?

Many supervisors don't understand why they remain in their present positions and aren't considered for promotions. They erroneously believe that they haven't prepared themselves enough for their next promotion. The real reason is that there's no one capable of taking over the responsibilities of his/her present position! Supervisors should make sure there's someone (possibly more than one) available to take over their present position. They should make sure that:

a) They have at least one "heel-nipper" snapping at their heels striving for their position. It's the supervisor's responsibility to make sure that someone IS ready to take over their position. They can accomplish this by developing the skills and abilities of potential subordinates. Accomplish this by putting them into acting positions, giving them proper training and allowing them to use that training (at least part of the time).
b) Make sure they are ready themselves for the next step up.

The Delegation Process

The supervisor:

a) Defines objectives. (What does s/he want to accomplish.)
b) Delegates responsibility and authority to subordinate;

c) Develops standards of performance for tasks assigned. Employee is held accountable to their supervisor for the standards of performance for assigned tasks; and

d) Supervisor appraises completed tasks.

Delegation:

When delegating tasks - ask yourself:

1. Why is the task done this particular way? Employees may say, *"We've always done it this way."* Don't listen to this old cliché!

2. What exactly takes place in the completion of the task - what's the purpose of doing it?

3. When is the task being done? Is it the best time to do it? Should it be combined with other tasks? Should it be done before or after other tasks?

4. Where should the task be done? Are there better alternative sites?

5. Who does the task? Who should do it? Can a less skilled person do it? (Keep budgets down).

6. How is the task performed and why is it done this way? Can we get performance easier or faster?

These questions help supervisors use their key resources of material, money, equipment and people.

Note: If you've been doing something the same way for over a three-year period, it's rather certain that some changes are in order.

When delegating tasks to individuals, the supervisor should:

a) Choose the right person to do the job.
b) Follow-up on progress.
c) Make sure staff meet their deadlines.
d) Encourage team effort.
e) Motivate employees by recognising jobs well done. Assist when problems occur.

45

Delegation Do's and Don'ts:

Do's:

- Delegate as simply and directly as possible. - Give precise instructions.
- Illustrate how each task applies to organisational goals.
- Mutually develop standards of performance.
- Clarify expected results.
- Anticipate what questions your employees may have and answer them.
- Discuss and resolve recurring problems.
- Seek out employees' ideas on how to do the job better.
- Stress the positive rather than the negative.
- Be supportive – exhibit trust.
- Recognise superior performance.
- Keep your promises.

Don'ts:

- Do a lot of the work yourself. Instead, delegate to your staff.
- Lie.
- Make promises you don't intend to keep.
- Keep your fingers out of employee's work - don't interfere or possibly compete with your employees.
- Expect too much from employees.
- Threaten your staff. Effective delegation depends more on leadership skills than coming from a position power.
- Assume a condescending attitude.
- Just give answers. Show how and why.
- Criticise employee in front of others.
- Give excessive checks on progress.

Sample Delegation Problem:

Six months ago, Roger Miln was promoted to the position of foreman - Plant Maintenance at the Billings Tool & Dye Company. He had been a mechanic on the company's maintenance force for almost twenty years.

Roger was a good worker, and everyone knew it. He enjoyed his work and thoroughly understood the operation, maintenance and repair of the many pieces of electrical and mechanical equipment used throughout the plant. Because of his technical competence, he had the respect of the rest of the crew, which was the main reason he was chosen as foreman.

Roger hadn't supervised people before. The Operations Manager (Jake Miller) told him that he would do much less of the actual work himself. Instead, he would be responsible for training and directing the work of the people under him.

At first, Roger tried to act the way he thought a supervisor should act. For example, he started wearing a tie every day to work, so he could look the part. He tried to organise his day so he could spend most of it doing paperwork. It wasn't long however, before complaints started to come in from the production floor. Machinery was breaking down which held up production because repairs weren't being made fast enough.

When Roger sent his men to make repairs, they often called back to him for help because they didn't know how to fix the equipment themselves. Sometimes Roger could help matters by giving directions over the phone, but more often than not, he went down and did the job himself.

Gradually, Roger spent more and more time away from his desk and soon he was back in his work clothes. He felt as if things went better when he was there himself. He felt hard pressed to keep the equipment running and keep up with the growing workload.

Roger's crew started grumbling that he was too possessive with the machinery. They claimed he was deliberately not showing them how to do the work because he liked to do it himself.

Jake Miller talked to Roger several times about the situation. After each talk, Roger spent more of his time supervising and less time doing tasks, then would slip back into doing most of the tough jobs himself.

In the face of the continuing complaints from production, Jake knew he had to act, but didn't know what to do. He realised that Roger was an excellent mechanic, but also realised he wasn't adequately performing his supervisory duties.

Before peeking at the answers, see if you can answer the following two questions:

Question #1: What was the problem?

Question #2: How could Jake solve the problem?

#1. What was the problem?

Most people identified the following as being the major problems:

1. Jake hadn't prepared or trained Roger properly to handle his new position as supervisor.
2. Roger wasn't training his staff properly so they could take over many of the duties he was now doing.

Many people miss the most important problem (at least in the eyes of the employer Billings Tool & Dye). If *you* owned the company - what would you think was the major problem?

(Remember that the major objective of business is - making money). The answer is:

3. Production was down because the machines weren't being maintained properly.

#2. How could Jake Miller solve the above problems?

To solve the production problem, Jake and Roger needed to work very closely to make sure that the machines were maintained properly, and all the other tasks were completed. Next, Jake needed to take time to train Roger properly or send him to a supervisory skills course of some kind. Then, Roger needed guidance himself on how to train his staff, so they could take over some of his duties and do more of the maintenance work.

Another area that most supervisors missed is that whoever was in the Supervisory position before Roger hadn't prepared Roger for the supervisor's job. This is why it fell on Jake Miller (the manager of the area) to take over the training responsibilities of the former supervisor.

Jake sent Roger to a course on supervision. At the same time, he coached Roger on how to train his people. At the start, instead of doing the work himself, Roger showed others how to do the maintenance and repairs. Soon his staff was taking over more and more of his work. Roger progressed from worker to teacher, coach and finally supervisor and occasional "technical consultant."

The shirt and tie became his permanent dress, and he liked it! Jake realised that Roger's technical knowledge was most valuable when he passed it on to his people. Roger had the capacity to supervise - he just lacked the know-how to do it.

Demotions:

Had you thought that Roger might be sorry that he'd accepted his supervisory promotion? Did you decide that Jake should let him go back to his original position? Be careful in cases like this. Check the laws in your area before you contemplate demoting an employee. If an employee is demoted, some laws state that it's comparable to being fired by the company and re-hired at a lower-level position. If the employer doesn't have documentation to prove that the employee had unsatisfactory performance, they could be charged with Wrongful Dismissal.

However, there is a way to deal with this situation safely, so that the employer would be covered if there were any possible repercussions. If Roger wanted to go back to his original position, he should be asked to put his request in writing. This dated and signed documentation would be placed on his personnel file. Only then is the company safely covered if they demoted him.

Standards of Performance:

Many delegation problems begin because the employee simply doesn't know what their supervisor expects of them. This could be because there's either no position description available or a very poorly written or out-dated one.

Position descriptions and performance appraisals should both have detailed standards of performance to clarify what is expected of employees.

A Standard of Performance is a yardstick against which performance in a particular part of a job is measured. It's usually a series of brief statements about the quality and quantity expected within specific time frames.

For example:

Task: To hire three sales personnel
Standard of Performance:
To hire three sales personnel who have a minimum of three years' directly related experience by May 1, 20____, at a salary range of $40,000 to $45,000 per annum.

Quality: - 3 years' directly related experience. (You'd have to establish what "directly related experience" really means).
Quantity: - 3 sales personnel
Time: - By May 1, 20___.
Cost: - Salary range of $40,000 to 45,000 per annum.

When setting Standards of Performance, consider:

a) The performance of other people in similar situations. (Watch you don't choose a high or low achiever's performance as "average!")

b) Engineered or prevailing standards.

c) Employees' past performance on the job as shown from their previous performance appraisals.

d) What supervisors and employees negotiate as reasonable.

Advantages of setting Standards of Performance:

A worker, who knows his or her job has certain specific standards, is always aware of how s/he is doing. Employees can rate their own job effectiveness and start improvement in unsatisfactory areas without waiting for appraisals from their supervisors.

Standards of Performance enable the supervisor to evaluate his or her whole department realistically. Supervisors can spot areas where individual employees need improvement, take steps to improve the whole group and recognise superior performance.

Standards make it possible to base performance rating on something more objective than personality traits and surface impressions. They keep the personalities out of it and deal only with the actual output of the employee.

Position Descriptions:

Position descriptions should include all the information you'd want, if you were filling the position. Remember, that Position Descriptions describe the position - not the person filling it.

Some sample headings on a job description are:

- Title of Position:
- Position #:
- Location:

- Hours of work:
- Department, branch, or unit:
- Reports to:
- Job Summary: (in paragraph form - just giving a brief description of the position).
- Duties and Responsibilities: (showing percentage of time spent on each duty or weighting in importance.)
  Start with **Key Performance Indicators** (KPIs). These are the major functions of the job.
  For instance:
  KPI: Responsible for all company training.
  Under each KPI, list all the tasks that must be performed to achieve the KPI. For instance: Ensure that all supervisors and managers receive our approved 3-day supervisory training course by June 1st, 20____ for a cost of less than $120,000.
  Under each task, list the standards of performance relating to that task.
  For example:
  Quality: Approved 3-day supervisory training course.
  Quantity: All supervisors and managers.
  Time: June 1st, 20____.
  Cost: Less than $120,000.
- Work Complexity: (such as choice of action, consequences of error, difficulty or work pressures, contacts, confidentiality).
- Supervision received: (level, how much independent action).
- Whom position supervises: (Titles of positions - direct or indirect supervision. Do they assign work? Review work? Conduct performance appraisals? Discipline subordinates?)
- Working conditions: (be specific about adverse conditions).
- Equipment used: (be specific).

- Qualifications required: such as formal education, experience, specific skills, licenses or certificates, physical requirements (i.e., The employee must be able to lift packages weighing up to 10 kg above his/her head).
- Probationary period:
- Promotional opportunities:

No more than 10% of their duties are to be identified as: "Other Duties as Assigned."

If the employee performs the duty every day, every week or once every year – it should be on his or her position description.

Why is probationary period included on a position description? While an employee is on probation, there's far less paperwork should you wish to fire them because of inadequate performance. The employee would probably want to know how long the probationary period is, because many companies don't put employees on full company benefits until their probationary period is over.

How long should a probationary period be? Most companies have anywhere from three months to one year. If employees have to wait a full year to receive company benefits (which can be 30 to 50% of their base salary) they'd miss a lot of extra money. It's also a long time to be on "tender-hooks" wondering if they're going to be accepted as a full-time employee. Some union agreements stipulate set probationary periods.

Promotional opportunities need to be listed as well. If candidates are "fast-trackers" you'll lose them if they're placed in a dead-ended position with little chance of promotion. On the other hand, many people are not "fast trackers" and would be content staying in one position for a long time.

Knowing your employees better:

A company's most valuable asset is its people. Unless you know your staff well, you're probably not going to take advantage of their unique talents and abilities. You can get to know your staff much better by going over their resume or application form with them. Even if your staff have worked for you for three years, there are likely things they've done in the past that you're unaware of. You'd find this information on their application form and/or resume.

After discussing his/her history, go over the position description with them. If there isn't one - do the following:

Give your subordinate a position description form and ask them to complete it. Train them how to establish standards of performance. You would list the pertinent information and the KPIs, but leave the tasks and standards of performance for them to fill in. At the same time, complete one yourself. Then call a meeting and compare the two descriptions. They're seldom the same. You might also determine the following with your employee's assistance:

a) Which tasks are the most important (what you think are most important may not be the same as those the employee chooses!)

b) How much time do you spend on each task? Work out in percentages and put next to the task.

c) Which duties would you classify as routine duties? Which are periodic duties (once a week, a month etc.) or special projects?

d) Which tasks do you enjoy the most and why? Ask this because you'll know who's likely to be the best qualified to handle a new project. The likelihood of a good job being done is higher if the employee enjoys the tasks they're doing.

e) Which tasks do you dislike the most and why? You will probably have to watch over employee more closely because you'll know they dislike this kind of task. You may consider delegating tasks of this nature to someone else who doesn't have this particular dislike.

f) Which tasks do you feel should be handled by someone else? It's possible that the employee is doing step two of a process, while another does step one and three. They may feel (and they could be right) that it would be better if one person handled all three steps.

g) Which tasks do you feel should be assigned to you, but aren't? It's possible they are the ones doing step one and three, and also feel that they should be doing step two as well.

h) Is there anything you can do to help them complete their tasks more efficiently?

You may find some unexpected information turns up when you discuss the above questions. In the end, you'll have a job description that's accurate and an employee who knows what s/he's expected to do.

Analysing Your Supervisory Job:

This will help you to analyse what you are doing on your job. Take a piece of paper and answer the following:

1. How much of your time do you usually spend doing actual work? _____%. How much time do you spend supervising your staff? _____%.
2. Note below any "work" you are doing yourself that you should be passing on to others.
3. Who could you give this work to? (List their names).
4. What kind of training or coaching do they need to do the work correctly?
5. What work do you do for people when help is needed?
6. How could you coach or explain instead?
7. How much input do you give to your staff on how they complete their tasks?

How can you encourage your people to develop their own ideas? (Relating to question 7):

What do you normally do when an employee asks for advice? Do you automatically give them the answer? Do they seem to rely on you too much? Do they depend on you to make even small decisions for them?

If this is the case try the following:

When they ask you a question, return their comments with a question of your own, *"What do you think you should do?"* Many of your employees know what they should do - all you need to do is confirm that they're correct. This gives them confidence in their own decision-making capabilities. Soon they'll be making more of their own decisions that will allow you to spend time on more constructive tasks.

Do you delegate enough to your staff? The following questions may shed some light on the subject. Answer honestly (the way things are, not how you would like them to be).

How Much Do I Delegate?

On paper, ask yourself the following questions (answering with "yes" or "no:"

1. Have I taken all vacations in the past five years (Are you afraid to delegate?)
2. Do I work longer hours than those reporting to me? (Is this really necessary?)
3. Do I usually do company work at home?
4. Do I get more than two business-related phone calls a week at home?
5. Do I frequently come into the office when it's closed? (It's often quiet between 7 and 8 a.m.)
6. Am I usually behind in my work?
7. Do I measure my success primarily by time worked, rather than by accomplishment?
8. Do my people request advice more than once or twice a day? (Ask them what *they* think they should do).
9. Do I have limited time for outside interests?

10. Are position descriptions for my people of the activity type? (Prepares, responsible for, etc.)
11. Does the organisational chart for my unit accurately reflect responsibility and reporting status?
12. Do my people consistently make recommendations to me? (They often provide the best suggestions).
13. Do my employees know specifically the results they must reach?
14. Are my staff consistently ready for promotions?
15. Have I reserved too many tasks strictly for myself?
16. Have I clearly defined authority? In writing?
17. Am I the kind of boss I'd like to report to?
18. How many times have I over-ruled my employees in the past year?
19. How often do I check on their work?
20. How many staff meetings do I hold a month?
21. Do I reward and discipline based on results, not on how they do the job?
22. Do I give clear, concise directions to my staff?
23. Do my staff misunderstand my directions more than expected?
24. Are important decisions postponed when I'm away?
25. Do I call my office when I'm on holidays?
26. Does anyone schedule appointments for me?
27. Do I really know the strengths and weaknesses of my people?
28. Do I make changes affecting them without giving them the reasons why the change is necessary?
29. Could I delegate more tasks than I do?
30. Do I realise that unless someone is trained to take over my position, I will be passed over for my next promotion?

This exercise will be a waste of time unless you go over it carefully and determine what you're willing to do to correct any deficiencies identified.

Once you've delegated a task to an employee - how do you motivate them to do a good job?

CHAPTER FOUR

MOTIVATION

Motivation:

The expression "different strokes for different folks" fits motivation as well. You may not be able to motivate some employees at all. Identifying the wants and needs of employees is a major task faced by most supervisors.

Motivation - like bathing - must be done on a regular basis to be effective.

Don't let employees use negative terms to describe what they do for your company. For instance, *"I'm only a receptionist ... janitor ... clerk, etc."* Explain why their position is crucial to the smooth running of your company. Give examples of what would be the repercussions if they fail to complete their tasks properly.

What motivates most employees?

Make a list of the things you believe really motivate employees. See how many you've observed in the workplace.

Each employee has a different set of values and priorities. Try to hit their "hot button" then watch the difference in their performance. As different jobs attract different people, motivation is often very personal to an individual. Here are many that you could choose from, depending on the employee you're trying to motivate:

Money. Many feel this is the only thing that would really motivate employees. For some this is true, but for the majority, not true. Often the opportunity of making more money can be the motivator (a possible promotion).

Recognition. This is probably the best motivator of all. It's very high on employees' lists of things that truly motivate them. Recognition for a job well done seems to be the incentive for more favourable behaviour that in turn allows them to receive more recognition. A well-timed pat-on-the-back can turn around even the most lethargic, aggressive or demanding employee. If you want even more impact, put your praise down on paper, so the recipient can save it and read it whenever s/he wishes.

Seniority. Employees receive special company benefits because of long-term employment. This could be a bigger office, more company benefits, a company car, etc. This can de-motivate other more conscientious or high-achieving employees who see seniority as a negative reason for recognition and more money.

Merit System. This would make sure that employees would receive a salary related to their productivity, rather than their seniority in their company. This eliminates much of the "deadwood" in corporations. Those who've always expected their company to protect their employment simply because they've worked for the company for a long time fear this method.

Status. This would be in the title of the position or the employee's perceived importance to the company. For instance, would you prefer the title Junior Clerk or Input Worker? I'm sure you'll agree that Input Worker sounds much more important. An employee is less reluctant to give his/her title, if they were asked, *"What do you do for a living?"*

Challenge. The opportunity to grow, to stretch, to use their full potential is the motivator for many. The idea of winning is a definite turn-on to many who enjoy the gamble.

Competition. To those with a competitive nature (most sales types) competition is a definite turn-on to higher productivity. They thrive on the excitement of the challenge.

Security. For employees who believe their jobs are in jeopardy (or those waiting for a pending lay-off) letting them know that their job is secure (and the company is solvent) may be the only motivator they need to do a good job.

Lack of Security. If your job is on the line because of poor productivity or behaviour, you'll likely clean up your act and produce more (shape up - or ship out procedure). This is a negative motivator but may be the only motivator for your lazier employees or those who lack direction and goals.

Responsibility. Doing only part of the job, can be a turn-off to employees. When employees have the full responsibility for the completion of a task, they feel a much higher sense or achievement. They say, *"I was the one in charge of **that** project. My boss said I did a good job."*

Promotional Opportunities. This is a turn-on to the high achiever or someone who really wants to get ahead in a hurry. For those who are at the minimum wage level, it can be an incentive to work harder, so they can earn more money.

Training. When companies give training to their employees, staff feel as if their companies care about them and are interested in their well-being. Companies that utilise manpower planning will use training to make sure their existing staff are ready for promotional opportunities. They encourage development of talents and abilities and allow employees to use their training and experience.

Achievement. Many companies make public announcements when their employees accomplish something unexpected. *"I'd like to congratulate Bill Martin who was able to obtain XYZ Company as a client. We've been trying to obtain this prestigious client for many years and Bill was able to pull it off. Congratulations Bill."*

Awards. Companies give perfect attendance awards, sales awards, charity awards and give recognition for work above and beyond the call of duty.

Extra privileges. Employers might decide that employees can go home when they complete their allotted work.

Additional benefits. This could include a company car, expense account, a corner office, own personal assistant, company credit card, season's tickets to concerts or sporting events or the use of a condominium in Hawaii, etc.

Leadership style of supervisor. A good leader can motivate employees to give their best effort, simply because they respect their leader and want to do their best for him/her. In return they want their supervisor to be proud of them.

Hours of work. Companies that implement flex time find it to be a great motivator. Their early risers (morning people) could start at 7:00 am and leave at 3:00 pm. Late starters would start work at 10:00 am and leave at 6:00 pm.

Job sharing. This occurs when two employees share the responsibilities of one (normally full-time) position. Some split the duties with one person working in the morning, another in the afternoon. Salaries and benefits are also split in half. In other cases, the employees may work two days one week and three the next. It's an ideal set-up for working mothers, those with second jobs or those close to retirement.

Company Social Events. The opportunity for workers to associate with each other socially is a good motivator for some employees. This could be having a company baseball team, bowling night, company picnic, barbecue, or other social event.

The work itself. Job rotation often reduces the boredom of repetitive kinds of tasks. There's another spin-off benefit - that of having more than one person qualified to take over the duties of a position. If an employee is on vacation or ill, another can take over their duties reducing any backlog. When supervisors know the talents and abilities of their staff, they can delegate work to those who appear to like that kind of task. Giving employees new tasks that keep them learning, will also remove the tedium of their work.

Supervisors should resist hiring either over- or under-qualified staff. Over-qualified staff will likely be bored with their job within months. If you've made this faux pas, the employee will probably want a promotion in a hurry. You may lose them to another company unless you allow them that opportunity.

Under-qualified staff will be playing the game of "catch-up" which could be very stressful for them. You'll have to give them extra training and time to catch up with the position expectations. Consider extending their probationary period longer than normal, so you have more opportunity to see if they can handle the position before making them permanent employees.

Working Conditions. This is very high on the list for many employees. Anything you can do to make working conditions better, will repay your company's investment with increased productivity and higher employee morale. There are many things that companies can do to improve working conditions:

Noise. If employees are working against deadlines, they're likely under some stress. Anyone who's under stress suffers from the "fight or flight syndrome." This is their instinctive behaviour when under stress that prepares them to fight their way out of a predicament or to run away. When this happens, their five senses become more sensitive.

When under stress, hearing becomes much sharper. This is why (when you're under stress) you jump when someone makes a loud noise and why companies try to reduce noise. These efforts include installing rugs, placing acoustic tiles in ceilings, use raised wall-coverings (such as matted wallpaper) and provide dividers between work stations. They turn telephone bell levels down or provide soft background music.

Lighting - either too much or too little. When under stress, the pupils dilate (so the person can better see the beast that's stalking them.) Far too many offices have four bars of fluorescent lights in one spot. This is far too many. When there are this many lights together, it provides a glare that is extremely hard on the eyes, often causing eyestrain and/or headaches. Employees are squinting their eyes by late afternoon. This glare is similar to sitting in a boat on a bright sunny day without sunglasses. The fluorescent light hits light surfaces (such as white paper) and reflects upward into the eyes of the worker (like the water does in a boat). Many employees have to wear tinted glasses to cut out the glare. A more sensible solution is to remove two of the fluorescent tubes. Even better - replace them with two orange-coloured soft fluorescent bulbs rather than the white ones.

Working position.

Standing. Those who have to stand for long periods of time should have something to rest one of their feet on, that alternates the weight-bearing leg. At one time grocery store clerks could only work three to four hours at a time. Their employer believed that the lifting of articles and the packaging of groceries was the reason. When one of the large grocery stores had their cashiers stand on half-inch rubber mats, they found they could work for much longer. The same concept was used where employees moved back and forth along a long counter. Companies find that employees' back and leg problems are drastically reduced. Because most businesses have concrete floors with no resiliency, the provision of rubber mats or rugs with deep underlay affords this same benefit.

Sitting. Watch most employees when they're deeply engrossed in what they're doing. Most of them sit on the edge of their chairs. This doesn't let them take advantage of the back-saving support of their chairs. Make your staff aware of what they're doing and remind them to use this support.

Companies should condemn most secretarial chairs. Have you ever sat in one? Try leaning back. What happens? Right - you would probably tip the chair over backwards along with yourself. This is ludicrous when you figure the hours most support staff spend in those chairs. Companies should provide them with the same kind of chairs with arm rests their bosses have, only smaller to fit into the narrower space most have at their desks. This will support their arm when they are using a mouse.

Word Processors/computers. Word processors and computers can cause not only neck strain but also eye strain if they're placed in the wrong position. The screen should be set at a comfortable height. Employees should not be looking upward towards their screen, but rather their eyes should be almost parallel with the top of the screen.

Be observant of the lighting around the screen. If there's a window behind the worker, it will reflect glare on the screen. The employee's eyes will then have the double problem of adjusting to the reflected light and the information shown on the screen. This is also true if light is hitting or reflecting on the screen from either side. If there happens to be a window behind the screen, the worker's eyes will again be in trouble because of the direct light coming from the window. The ideal situation is to have light barriers set up in such a way that the screen has no reflected light at all. Providing non-glare screens is a definite asset.

Proper temperature. Most offices have a constant battle between the male employees who wear heavy wool suits and the female employees wearing lighter apparel. Often men want the office cooler and women want more heat. Unless the working environment is comfortable for all workers, they may not be as productive as they should be.

Colour. Colour has a definite bearing on the ability of staff to do a good job. One warehouse had all the walls and shelving painted grey. Their employees' moods seemed to match. They decided to re-paint their walls a creamy-yellow and their shelves a different colour for each section. It was soon apparent that this made a definite difference in the productivity and morale of their staff. It was also easier to find products because of the colour coding, *"It's the third shelf of the blue shelving."*

Plants. These provide a soothing atmosphere and soften the glare of concrete and steel.

Furniture. Wooden furniture appears softer, more pleasing and less serious than steel.

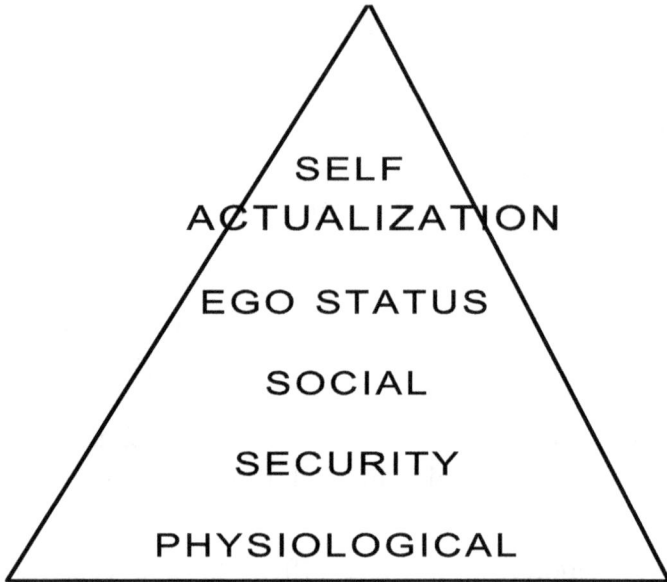

```
         SELF
    ACTUALIZATION
     EGO STATUS
       SOCIAL
      SECURITY
    PHYSIOLOGICAL
```

Maslow's Hierarchy of Needs

Mazlow's Hierarchy of needs can be very effective to help you motivate different employees:

Physiological Needs:

These include the fundamentals of survival, including hunger and thirst. Until this need is met, the four others won't likely be motivators. Money (or the lack of it) is what motivates most at this level.

High absenteeism and turnover are the results when these needs are not met. Proper temperature, tolerable noise level and a comfortable body position are important.

Supervisors might not be able to provide more money to their staff, but they can motivate employees by giving them recognition for a job well done and making them aware of promotional opportunities. Improving working conditions will likely help these employees do a better job and job rotation can help alleviate boredom.

Security Needs:

This is the employee's need for safety. The employee wants to continue his/her physiological needs, but seeks protection against danger, illness and loss of his/her job or other threats to security. If a person feels his/her job is in jeopardy, s/he will stop taking risks - will walk the middle-line and become an average or poor performer.

Supervisors must be on top of this situation and deal with conditions that appear to threaten the security of their staff. If staff fear a pending lay-off (and none is imminent) make sure they know this is not going to happen. If your staff is afraid of being replaced because of new technology - allay their fears about being replaced. Keep aware of their anxieties and try to alleviate them as soon as possible. Be proactive - not reactive.

Those who have obtained written warnings on their file will feel their security is threatened. They'll stop taking risks and may give only average performance (even though they're capable of much more).

Non-smokers forced to work in an environment that allows smoking, object to the security risk to their health. Many will leave a job because of this lack of security and safety.

When employees have met their physiological and security needs, others surface.

Social Needs:

This is the yearning to belong, to have friends and acquaintances, to be liked and accepted. Supervisors need to take steps to make newcomers feel part of a group. Employees, who work in a hostile atmosphere, seldom use teamwork when completing tasks, so supervisors must be on top of personality clashes. Many companies fill this need by providing social events for their employees to enjoy and socialise with each other.

Ego Needs:

This is the need for self-esteem and recognition received from others. To these individuals, status level is important, where the title of their position might be important - even more important than salary.

Employees must feel that others respect them and want their efforts recognised. If they're not, they'll channel their energies elsewhere (Is possibly a star bowler - expending more energy at social things). If supervisors channel this energy towards more productivity, they'll likely improve the ego of the employee as well.

Self-Actualisation:

Freed from the difficult task of satisfying external needs, people are now ready to explore their true selves. They can use their interests, talents, skills, knowledge and abilities to fulfil their highest potential as human beings.

Everyone benefits if a supervisor can get an employee to this level by meeting his/her motivational needs. This is why it's important to find your employee's "hot button." It's unfortunate, but approximately 80 percent of all employees are in the wrong job! You'll believe this if you ask people about their jobs. The ones who are happy (self-actualised) will describe their job in positive terms. Those who aren't self-actualised will use negative terms to describe what they do.

If a company doesn't recognise and use the potential of both its high and low achievers and attempt to motivate people, their employees may simply move elsewhere. Many find that they can only reach this level by being self-employed where they can use all their talents and abilities. A supervisor can provide this atmosphere by making employees feel as if they're working for themselves. Companies that offer stock options believe their employees feel more important. What they do on the job affects them directly, so their performance improves.

Altruism:

This is the stage after self-actualisation where the person's content to see him or herself self-actualised but wants others to reach this level as well. They usually forget competition and concentrate on developing the talents of others with little or no thought of pay. Many become mentors for junior staff who show promise.

Other examples of this are the auto mechanic who fixes his friends' cars in his spare time. Or the hairdresser who looks after the hair needs of all her friends. They love their job so much that they like to share their talents in their free time as well.

The Need Hierarchy at Work:

Here's how you can motivate people at the different levels:

Physiological Needs:

- Pleasant working conditions;
- More leisure time;
- More luxurious personal property;
- Avoidance of physical strain or discomfort; and
- More money as a means of providing basic comforts.

Security Needs:

- Fringe benefits;
- Safe working conditions; and
- Seniority protection.

Social Needs:

- Friendly colleagues;
- Opportunity for interaction;
- Harmonious interpersonal relations; and
- Team membership.

Ego Needs:

- Opportunities for advancement;
- Recognition based on merit (not seniority);
- Job assignments that allow display of skill;
- Inclusion in planning activities; and
- Status related to job title.

Self Actualisation:

- Involvement in innovative and active activities;
- Greater ego involvement;
- Increased investment of oneself in their work; and
- Freedom to make one's own decisions.

Herzberg's Theory:

Dr. Frederick Hertzberg has explained Maslow's theories and places emphasis on motivation. He identified two sets of factors that affect the way in which people react.

Hygiene Factors: Fall under Physiological and Security levels - Pay, benefits, working conditions, fringe benefits, supervision, interpersonal relations, rules and policies.

Motivators: Fall under Social, Ego Status and Self Actualisation - challenge, responsibility, recognition, achievement, opportunity for personal growth, advancement and the work itself.

The hygiene factors don't help a person to move past an average performance level. True motivators are those that cause a person to be happy with their jobs and thus more productive. These are added to the hygiene factors so employees can move out of the average performance level.

Unsatisfied needs are strong sources of de-motivation in the workplace. Supervisors should watch for these needs. By knowing their employees well, they'll learn what motivates each of them.

PROBLEM EMPLOYEES:

Do you have problem employees that you can't seem to motivate? Look over the above information and see if you can pick out how you've tried to motivate them so far. What other methods could you try that will motivate them?

George and Sam:

Here's a situation involving motivation. See if you can determine what you would do if you were the supervisor of these two employees:

George and Sam have the same level position and duties. George is a high achiever. He's upset that he and Sam have the same salary, yet he accomplishes much more than Sam and is accurate in his work. Sam is what George describes as an average to poor achiever (this is true).

Before looking at the following information - determine what you would answer to these two questions:

- How can you motivate George?
- How can you motivate Sam to reach George's high performance?

Here are your choices:

1. How can you motivate George?

(a) Should you introduce a merit system where high achievers like George are paid more than low achievers like Sam?

(b) Could George be ready for a promotion? If so, try to see what you can do for him.

(c) Give him time off? (When he completes his work, let him go home?)

(d) Could you use him to train Sam to bring up his production?

2. How can you motivate Sam to reach George's high performance?

a) Should you implement a merit system where high achievers like George are paid more than low achievers like Sam?

b) Is Sam bored, overqualified for his job, therefore ready for a promotion? You would have to let him know that his poor productivity is holding him back from a promotion.

c) Could Sam be under-qualified or under-trained to handle his duties or is he a new employee? His low productivity is then understandable. He should receive less salary than George. His starting salary should have been lower until he was fully trained. He could be given a raise at the end of his probationary period.

d) Could Sam have a health problem that is keeping him from full production?

e) Should Sam be demoted to a lower-level position? If this is your choice, be careful about the laws in your area. You may have to prove that he was unqualified to handle the duties of his old position, before placing him in a new one. This would include accurate, detailed documentation otherwise you could run into legal problems. In many instances the law sees this in the same light as someone who was fired and rehired at a lower level. You'd have to prove that the employee was incapable of handling his position, therefore had to be demoted to a lower-level position.

f) Could Sam be a slow-learner and is working at his full capacity?

The above situation would probably not have occurred if the company was using a merit system. You can't blame workers for being de-motivated when they see less talented (often less motivated) employees receiving the same salary as they are. This is one of the major faults of the seniority system. Employees become lethargic and don't put in the effort necessary to stay on top of their jobs.

When companies implement merit systems, their employees usually raise their production and quality levels. They know that unless they've given a dollar's worth of work, they won't receive a dollar's worth of pay. Those that don't follow this take the chance of being disciplined and/or fired.

Employee Problem:

Here's another example.

Harry Bailey has been with Davis Associates a little more than 8 months. During the first few months on the job, he was quite happy with his decision to come to work for Davis. Actually, at the time, he had considered himself lucky to get the job and looked forward to starting.

He was impressed with the interest the employment interviewer had taken in him. His supervisor seemed very competent in his interview with Harry.

Once on the job, it became apparent to Harry that the company was going to spend some money training him. The first three full days on the job, he spent learning about the equipment he was going to operate. There had even been a long orientation about the company and its products.

Things had gone rather well the first few months. His supervisor checked with him fairly often to see how he was coming along and usually gave helpful suggestions to make Harry's work easier. Lately though, Harry has had less of this type of contact with his supervisor. Within the past two months, Harry made a couple of recommendations for changes in the operation that seemed to annoy his supervisor.

In fact, Harry was now beginning to have second thoughts about the wisdom of coming to Davis Associates. It seemed as though a lot of his earlier training was being wasted. The way the job went, he didn't need to know much about the equipment. Although it really wasn't quite the case, he had the feeling that if he could read "on and off," that's all he needed to do his job.

After all, there was someone to check his procedures - somebody inspected the output. When he tried to re-arrange the schedule to get a more efficient run, his supervisor told him that scheduling was someone else's worry and to do his own work.

Harry has found himself watching the clock more and more lately and looking forward to the end of the day.

Determine what you would do (a) if you were Harry and (b) if you were his supervisor and found out the above was happening.

What has happened to Harry?

- He can't use his own initiative;
- Is probably overqualified for his job, ready for a promotion;
- Is de-motivated by his supervisor;
- Not using training;
- Is frustrated and angry;
- Is getting negative or no feedback from his supervisor;
- Seems to have lost contact with his supervisor; or

- Is the supervisor threatened by Harry?

How can his supervisor restore his interest in his job?

- He should be encouraged to express his feelings to his supervisor;
- Should ask for a promotion;
- Scheduling could possibly be part of his job;
- He could use the training he's received to be back-up to others when they're away or sick;
- His supervisor should clarify why Harry's ideas can't be used; and
- His supervisor should review the procedures of the area to see if they're reasonable.

Understanding Frustration:

We see a considerable amount of tension in some offices. This is due to frustration and anger. A "block" can cause this frustration and anger. A block is something that stands between a person's needs and the satisfaction of that need, which can cause frustration. If a block remains long enough, the frustration will likely turn into anger. Your supervisory style or the things you do may be causing frustration (and eventually anger) in your staff.

Causes of Employee Frustration/Anger:

Employee's Need:

The desire to be regarded as a competent, worthwhile person.

Blocks:
- Restrictive supervision;
- Lack of recognition;
- Monotonous work;
- Little opportunity to try new ideas;
- No new skill growth;

- Poor fit between abilities and job requirements.

Satisfaction of Need:

- Work that satisfies this desire.
- Praise and recognition from his supervisor.
- The opportunity to use and develop his talents and abilities.
- Rekindling his love for his job.

Restrictive Supervision

If you don't let your staff take an active part in how they complete their assignments, they're likely to obtain less job satisfaction. The more employees participate in how they do things, the more co-operative they'll be.

A supervisor who uses an authoritarian leadership style is setting him/herself up to fail.

Lack of Recognition

Supervisors de-motivate staff if they identify only the 2 percent their subordinates have done incorrectly, instead of concentrating on what the 98 percent they've done correctly.

Another pet peeve is that in the old "School of Management," supervisors believed it was their right to take credit for ideas suggested by their subordinates. As expected, this just de-motivates employees and discourages any new ideas. Progressive supervisors know that if they give employees credit where credit's due, they motivate their staff to perform better. This also alleviates mediocrity and marginal production.

Monotonous Work

When companies implement job rotation for their employees, they're attempting to make their employees' jobs more interesting. Job rotation involves several employees who work at substantially the same class or level of work and pay range.

Employers who use job rotation reap extra benefits because people can fill more than one job. Then, if employees are away sick, they're less likely to come back to work and face a mountain of work. If your company isn't doing this, suggest they try it!

Little Opportunity to Try New Ideas

Another prime de-motivator occurs when supervisors refuse to listen to their staff when they try to explain better ways of doing their work. If supervisors can't implement their ideas, at least they should explain why they can't.

No New Skill Growth

At one time, companies spent training dollars on their people and still couldn't keep up with the demand for competent qualified people. Recently companies have had to tighten their training budgets. Companies may refuse to give training that they believe employees can't use right away. Employees whose promotions are six months to one year away may find it difficult to obtain training.

Supervisors should encourage staff to obtain the training they need (on their own if necessary). The employee will reap benefits far beyond the costs they would invest in training. This gives the employee an edge over others who have not obtained this training on their own.

Poor fit between abilities and job requirements

Before the economic downturn, many employees projected that they would climb the ladder in their companies very quickly. They now find they are over-qualified for their present positions. If the expected promotion is still far in the future, they may decide to move to another company.

Other staff members may be in the wrong kind of job, but don't know where to turn for help. These employees simply "put in time" on the job. If a supervisor notices this behaviour, they might be reluctant to suggest career counselling for them because they're afraid they might lose the employee. However, they'll likely lose them anyway and often career counselling can identify areas the staff member can move to in the future. They'll probably need to take night courses to prepare for their new career choice. In the meantime, they'll likely continue working for you while they're doing this. They'll be much more motivated to do a good job for you because of your caring attitude. You'll eventually lose them, but they'll be good workers in the meantime.

Common Ways We See Anger Expressed at Work:

1. **Direct "Take that;"**
    When faced with a frustrating condition at work, many employees respond by directly attacking the condition. This may develop new procedures proving the theory that "necessity is the mother of invention." However, if the frustrating condition continues, we're likely to see direct expressions of hostility that are destructive in intent. Or we may see some of the less direct.

    Example: An employee may know a faster, better way of completing a task, but the supervisor won't let him/her do it his/her way. They can become disgruntled, and their productivity level will suffer. They become "middle of the road" employees who appear to have tunnel vision.

2. **Sabotage "Let's get back at them;"**
    Sabotage in the workplace usually takes a much milder form than we typically associate with this word. Yet subtle forms of sabotage at work are very common. The work slow-down, the omitted procedure or the small error, are all evidence of the frustration-anger model at work.

    Example: A personal assistant intentionally makes lousy coffee, because she feels it's not her responsibility. (This task should have been listed on her job description along with standards of performance on how the task should have been completed).

3. **Over-compliance "If that's what you want ...:"**

One excellent way of expressing anger at the frustrating boss is to do exactly what s/he asks regardless of the circumstances. The boss can't fault this practice, because after all, it's what s/he said. But s/he didn't mean to be taken so literally! When a union wants to make life difficult for management, members start going by the letter, rather than the spirit of the contract (work-to-rule).

Example: You've given an employee a set of instructions on how to complete a project. You assume s/he'll use his/her common sense and add pertinent information necessary to complete the assignment. S/he didn't - the report is useless.

4. **Emotional withdrawal "They aren't that important:"**

One way to deal with continuing frustration is to deny the importance of the blocking conditions. This is the familiar "sour grapes" attitude. We often see employees become apathetic and just "go through the motions" on the job (nine to fivers). Their actions say, this job isn't that important (so just put in time). The really important things for them are outside the job (hate their jobs). If the interest and energy many workers spend on becoming star bowlers could be rekindled on the job, productivity gains would be considerable. Do this kind of employee a favour and encourage them to obtain career counselling to help them find out what job they want.

Example: An employee follows her job description to a "T." You, as her supervisor, know she's capable of much more.

5. **Turning inward "It must be me":**

One pathetic result of prolonged frustration is the tendency of some to turn their anger inward upon themselves. It can also happen when employees have written warnings on their file or have been demoted.

79

Instead of venting their anger against the blocking conditions through direct or indirect means, the individual begins to attack him or herself. S/he winds up with a feeling of *"I'm no good."* Turning such a person around is an immense supervisory challenge.

Example: An employee who has taken a risk and has been "burned" - may retreat into themselves and refuse to make decisions - use tunnel-vision in completing assignments - won't take risks - must feel safe in any decision they make.

Keeping Alive Employee's Desire to Contribute:

1. An atmosphere of approval:

A company can create an atmosphere of approval by observing the following steps:

(a) Recognise the importance of employee suggestions;

(b) Avoid "Progress Killers." For example:

- It isn't in the budget.
- We tried that before.
- It doesn't fit our program.
- Has anyone else tried it?
- It's against our policy.
- It costs too much.
- The union will scream.
- Management will scream.
- Employees will never buy it.
- We don't have the authority.
- Not that again!
- Let's give it more thought.
- We're all right without it.
- We've always done it this way!

(c) Explain why new ideas can't - or won't work. If employee gives a good idea - implement it as soon as possible and make sure to give the employee credit for the idea.

2. Meaningful participation:

The evidence is pretty convincing that whenever people can influence their own work and have a decisive voice; they'll be more interested and involved. Employees will feel their participation is meaningful if you practice the following:

(a) Analyse your job and decide which tasks you can move downward.

(b) Be willing to take the risk of more job involvement by your subordinates.

(c) Encourage your employees to volunteer for assignments you agree they can handle.

(d) Don't con your employees with the feeling that they're giving meaningful participation when you've already made a decision.

(e) When your decision is influenced by the employee's ideas - tell him/her.

3. Performance feedback:

Some supervisors (and thank goodness they're getting fewer and fewer) believe that the yearly performance appraisal is all that's necessary for the employee to perform properly. Of course, along the way they believe they should correct their employee if s/he does something wrong, but otherwise they're "on their own." Employees who work for this kind of supervisor usually find:

(a) They don't have an adequate position description.

(b) They aren't sure what's expected of them; therefore, have no objectives to meet.

(c) They seldom hear about what they did right (except silence) but appear to hear lots about what they did wrong.

4. Consistent discipline:

If supervisors show favouritism or have a personality clash with an employee, consistent discipline is usually a mirage. To guarantee consistent discipline a supervisor must:

(a) Review rules and standards periodically to evaluate their relevancy to current situations.
(b) Make sure all employees know the rules.
(c) Reward or punish consistently.
(d) Be aware of extenuating circumstances.
(e) Document your action and the reasoning behind your decision.
(f) Follow-up to see if the situation has improved.

Note: See my book *Easy Come - Hard to Go - the Art of Hiring Disciplining and Firing Employees* for information on this topic.

5. Right of appeal:

Used by the supervisor and the employee only after they have made serious attempts to settle a dispute. The third person or mediator is usually the Human Resources Manager, union representative or any trained negotiator who can remain objective about the conflict.

Companies that don't offer the "Right of Appeal" (which are usually non-union firms) are missing a very effective management tool. Sometimes, in a non-union environment, when an employee and their supervisor disagree on an important issue, the employee simply gives up and leaves the company. This may be a valuable employee, but the situation was such that they felt they would never be able to solve the situation. This is why companies need to recognise that employees and supervisors alike require an impartial person to intervene and help them settle their disputes.

6. Supervisors and managers should remember:

    (a) They're not always right - appeal procedures protect your staff from a supervisor's occasional lapses into biased opinion.

    (b) Ensure they listen effectively to their employee's reasoning behind their actions.

    (c) If they and their employee can't agree - involve another impartial third party.

    (d) Be willing to change their mind.

    (e) Welcome this appeal method as an aid rather than a threat. Remember, you too will have access to this management tool with *your* boss!

Performance Appraisals:

Does your company offer regular performance appraisals? What are these appraisals evaluating - employees' actual performance or such things as:

- judgement;
- initiative;
- attitude;
- interpersonal skills;
- conduct;
- reliability;
- customer relations;
- product knowledge;
- appearance;
- organisational ability;
- planning ability;
- quality of work;
- dependability;
- job knowledge;

- acceptance of criticism;
- responsibility level;
- motivation;
- persistence;
- independence;
- dedication.

Do you think these kinds of performance appraisals are effective? Are they fair? They can't be - because they're subjective - not objective. That kind of an evaluation would depend on whether the evaluator got up on the right side of the bed or not. The employee wouldn't know what to expect at performance appraisal time.

Here's how my copyrighted performance appraisal system works. I'm rather biased, but I believe it's one of the best available, because not only does it evaluate employees honestly, but removes the subjectivity from employee evaluations. It evaluates how well employees reach measurable objectives. Along the way, employees know exactly where they stand and there are no surprises at performance appraisal time. To be fair, supervisors must know how to set standards of performance upon which to evaluate their employees (covered in Chapter 3). Copies of this appraisal go to the employee, supervisor, personnel file, and union representative (if applicable).

If you wish to use our copyrighted performance appraisal for your company, please contact Cava Consulting,

cavaconsulting@ozemail.com.au

How Often Should Performance Appraisals Be Completed?

Many companies conduct performance appraisals when employees complete their probationary period. After that, it's done once a year - usually on the employee's anniversary date. Other companies conduct performance appraisals at the same time for every employee. Another company may have performance appraisals for each large special project their employees may complete (for example engineering or accounting firms).

Lee Iacoca asserts that all employees should have a performance appraisal quarterly. He believes that putting details down on paper makes a supervisor be more specific. It also:

1. Allows the person to be his/her own boss – to help set his/her own goals.
2. Makes employees more productive and motivated.
3. Encourages new ideas.
4. Keeps people from being buried or lost in the system.
5. The good guys don't get passed over.
6. The bad guys don't get to hide.
7. It improves communication between the supervisor and employees. The more employees set their own goals, the more likely they will react positively. If they don't measure up, the employee knows they've failed before the review. There are no surprises. Employees are often their own worst critics.

Pet Employees:

Supervisors sometimes pick a "pet" employee who seems to get away with murder, while others (those they can't get along with) get blamed for trivial things. Ask yourself if you have a "pet" employee. How about one that gets on your nerves? Don't be ashamed if you discover these human frailties about yourself, just stop when you find yourself displaying these negative tendencies. Treat all employees fairly.

Job Enrichment/Enlargement:

Many companies have had to downsize and now four people do the work that five used to do. There is a vast difference between this situation and job enrichment:

Job Enrichment: Is the development of talents, use of training, offering variety on the job, such as job rotation.

Job Enlargement: Is more of the same kind of task. Four people end up doing the work that five used to do. Another name for this is "job dumping."

How well do you motivate your staff?

Choose the appropriate number for each question.

a)   My people understand the reasoning behind current practices and procedures.

   1 = Rarely
   2 = Occasionally
   3 = Sometimes
   4 = Usually
   5 = Always

b)   The last time I listened closely to a suggestion from my people was:

   1 = I can't remember
   2 = 2 months ago
   3 = A month ago
   4 = Last week
   5 = Within last 2 days

c)   My employees' work is high in job enrichment.

   1 = Not really
   2 – Some are
   3 = So so
   4 = More than most
   5 = Definitely yes

d)   I let my people participate in decisions directly affecting them unless compelling reasons prevent it.

   1 = Rarely
   2 = Occasionally
   3 = Sometimes

4 = Usually

5 = Always

e) We discuss the rules we live by to see if revision is needed.

1 = Rarely

2 = Occasionally

3 = Sometimes

4 = Usually

5 = Always

f) Some of my people have accused me of "favouritism."

1 = Frequently

2 = More than most

3 = Sometimes

4 = Rarely

5 = Not to my knowledge

g) My people know where they stand.

1 = No, they don't

2 = Some do

3 = Most of them do

4 = Practically all

5 = Most of the time

h) I recognise good performance.

1. = Paycheque does it

2. = Sometimes I do

3. = More often than not

4. = Usually

5 = Always when observed

i) I encourage my people to express disagreement with my views if I'm dealing in a controversial area.

1. = Never

2. = Rarely

3. = Sometimes

4. = Fairly often

5. = Typically yes

1. My people know and feel free to use the right of appeal procedure (formal or informal) we have established.

    1 = No
    2 = Have procedures, but not widely known
    3 = Some
    4 = Most
    5 = Yes!

Total your score and check the climate ahead:

0 - 15 - Stormy Weather

16 - 34 - Changing

35 - 50 - Fair Skies

Any questions you have answered 1, 2 or 3 are negative - therefore require improvement. Put a * in the margin of those you wish to improve and set goals to reach those objectives.

Now that you've learned how to motivate your employees, you'll have to manage time properly so you can make good use of everyone's time.

CHAPTER FIVE

TIME MANAGEMENT

The Busy Man:

Here's a little poem I found that explains time management in a very effective way. (Author Unknown)

"If you want to get a favour done by some obliging friend,
And want a promise safe and sure on which you may depend,
Don't go to him, who always had much leisure time to plan,
But if you want your favour done, just ask the busy man.

The man of leisure never has a moment he can spare;
He's busy "putting off" until his friends are in despair;
But he whose every waking hour is crowded full of work,
Forgets the art of wasting time - he cannot stop to shirk.

So when you want a favour done and want it right away,
Go to the man who constantly works 20 hours a day.
He'll find a moment somewhere that has no other use,
And fix you while the idle man is framing an excuse."

A person from Mars would think time was something concrete they could put in their pockets and take back with them. We use statements such as:

- *"I don't have time."*
- *"Time is money."*
- *"Make time."*
- *"Save time."*
- *"Waste time."*
- *"Where did the time go?"*

- Referees call time.
- Prisoners serve time.
- Musicians mark time.
- Historians record time; and

- Loafers kill time.

As consumers, we often invest in labour-saving devices (which are really time-saving devices). Think of your grand or great grandmother. She likely washed clothes on a scrubbing board. Your grandmother or mother likely had a wringer washer. Now, you simply load the washing machine; add soap, push a button and everything is done for you.

And union and management discussions often concentrate on: shorter work week - flexible hours - overtime - double-time - full-time - permanent part-time, etc.

Time is important in today's society. We sense its importance and talk about it as if it was something concrete, we could see, feel and hold. Time is something that's limited to all of us. The minute that has just passed will never return to us. If you were eighty years of age, you'd know how valuable time is.

How we use the time we have - whether we waste it and just exist or whether we live each minute - depends on each one of us. How are you spending your valuable time? Are you in a rut and find yourself existing or are you living life to the fullest? Is it time to make some changes in your life?

Can you think of a person who's well organised? S/he's probably an effective time manager. Like many other things in life, effective time management is a skill anyone can learn. It's simply a matter of overcoming bad habits.

Areas of Life:

There are three basic areas of your life where you can use time management:

- Work or business life;
- Home or family life;
- Social or community life.

You'll need to control your time in all these areas to be truly happy. This balance can be put out of whack by unexpected

90

workloads or unwanted, dull or non-busy periods. I'm sure you can relate to the time when you had all day to complete an assignment and you goofed putting it together. You had too much time to complete it! I find that unless I get the momentum going first thing in the morning, I drag through the day.

Here are comments made about work time problems:

1. *"I have too much to do in my job."*
2. *"Everyone wants everything **now**!"*
3. *"I have no time to do the things I really want to do."*
4. *"Everything I do is halfway, not the way I'd like to complete tasks."*
5. *"I make mistakes because I hurry, and it frustrates me."*
6. *"My desk is never clear of things I'm supposed to do - I "just wish for once I could finish everything.*
7. *"I want to advance my career, but don't have time to learn the things I require for me to get to the next promotional level."*
8. *"I'm sure my boss isn't pleased with my work - because I'm not!"*

Do some of these cause problems for you?

When facing a distasteful task, promise yourself you'll give it fifteen minutes of hard effort. You'll probably find that the momentum you've started will probably keep you going until you finish the task.

Where do you have the most time problems? Is it at work or home (too many tasks to do)? Or does your social life suffer due to lack of time?

I offer three different time management seminars and find that most participants find they're so busy in their work and home life, that they neglect their social life. Watch this doesn't happen to you.

91

If you haven't let your "little kid" (your fun-side) out for a while, you may find you've lost your sense of humour. Please let your little kid out on a regular basis. This occurs when you let yourself have fun - with friends at a party, participating in a sport or playing with your children.

Principles of Time Management:

1. Every hour spent in effective planning saves three to four in execution and achieves better results. By failing to plan - you're planning to fail.
2. Daily planning, done either the afternoon before or early the same day, is essential for effective use of personal time.
3. Budget time to important and urgent tasks first.
4. Imposing deadlines on tasks or decisions and exercising self-discipline in adhering to them will aid in overcoming indecision and procrastination.
5. Keep a daytimer or "To Do" list and use it faithfully.
6. Be flexible in scheduling your time considering forces beyond your control.
7. Remember Murphy's Second Law, "everything takes longer than you think," and make allowances for this (especially when you delegate tasks to others).
8. Anticipatory action is usually more effective than remedial action. A stitch in time saves nine. Avoid surprises by expecting the unexpected and plan for it. Assume that if anything can go wrong, it will. (Murphy's Third Law).
9. People tend to over-estimate problems and treat all problems as if they were crises. Upon investigating these "crises" you'll probably find they're mostly low priority items to you.
10. Group similar tasks together. (i.e.: make all your phone calls at one time).

Time Log:

If you're having difficulties with #6, you probably haven't kept a time log to determine how much time you really spend on unexpected things. These could include unexpected telephone calls, interruptions and crisis.

Keep this log for a week so you can determine what percentage of your time you can count on for planned events. It could be that you're planning 60 percent of your day, when (because of unexpected events) you should only be planning 30 to 40 percent of your time.

Bottlenecks:

One problem some people confront is the bottleneck. Bottlenecks occur whenever a person fails to take essential action, because of indecision, laziness, mistaken priorities, stubbornness, overwork or because they procrastinate.

Supervisors are often guilty of this. If you don't delegate properly so your employees are busy all the time, *you're* probably the bottleneck in your area.

For example: You need to submit a month-end report and require information from other supervisors to complete it. If one of the supervisors doesn't complete his/her report on time, they're a bottleneck to you.

Different Kinds of Tasks:

Try to see which of these tasks cause you the most difficulty (possibly because there are so many of them):

1. **Simple short-term tasks:**
    These are routine activities found in any job. These tasks are simple and short-term in nature, which can occur frequently.
2. **Complex short-term tasks:**
    These are complex but require only short-time effort for accomplishment. They require an intermediate level of planning and effort.

3. **Simple long-term tasks:**
   These are simple but require long-term effort to complete. These tasks may also need an intermediate level of planning, due to the long-term effort required to complete them.
4. **Complex long-term tasks:**
   These take a high level of effort and planning. They're often avoided in favour of less complex tasks.

Did you identify either #1 or #3 as giving you the most problems? If these tasks are so simple - why aren't you delegating them downward? Could you pass some of those tasks on to your staff that would allow you to do the more important tasks you're paid to accomplish?

Swiss Cheese Approach:

Large blocks of uninterrupted time are a comparative rarity. If again and again (a few minutes before lunch, etc.) you choose to work on an unimportant task rather than begin a difficult important task - then you're procrastinating. You're avoiding what's really important.

One way to tackle complex long-term tasks is to use the Swiss Cheese approach (this is the cheese with holes in it). What you do is take "little bites" out of your long-term task. We call these little bites "instant tasks."

Instant tasks can take anywhere from one minute to an hour to accomplish. Most are five minutes or less. After each instant task, you would identify the time it would take to complete it.

For example: Your task is to hire 3 new employees. Several instant tasks would be:

1. Obtain the position description of the position: 2 minutes.
2. Write an ad for the newspaper advertisement: 15 minutes.
3. Screen one resume or application form: 5 minutes. (You would screen them all eventually.)
4. Set up one appointment: 5 minutes.

5. Conduct one interview: 45 minutes.
6. Evaluate one candidate: 7 minutes.

Using this method, you could fit in small instant tasks throughout your day as time permitted. For instance, if you were waiting for a phone call or had to go to a meeting in five minutes, you could screen one resume or application.

Complex Long-Term Assignment:

At my time management seminars, I give groups an assignment and ask them to identify instant tasks and work through the process. Here is the assignment I normally give them. The instant tasks you identify don't have to be sequential:

You're responsible for setting up your company's annual meeting (not their annual report). You can expect about 150 people to attend.

1. Choose several "Instant Tasks."
2. Set a time estimated to complete each task.
3. Determine obstacles you could run into while completing each task.

Here are some of the suggested "Instant Tasks."

1. Contact one hotel to see if they have facilities available when we want them. Also ask if they have accommodations for any out-of-town guests. Your next "Instant Task" could be to call another hotel.

   Time: 15 to20 minutes
   Obstacles: Person was not there, so you could not obtain the required information on first call.

   (Contacting all the relevant hotels would be a group of tasks. Contacting one of them would be an instant task.)

2. Arrange for audio-visual equipment.

   Time: 10 minutes

95

Obstacles: Equipment was not available in-house.

What is the one major thing you should do to accomplish the above task that will save you about 50 percent of your time? Suggestions you may make are:

a) Spend time planning;
b) Delegate tasks to others; or
c) Use a computer or word processor to record lists of tasks sequentially.

Most supervisors don't identify the most important task of all. What was the assignment? You were to set up your company's Annual meeting. This means that it's held every year. The major task you could do that would save 50 percent of your time is to find out who did it last year! Even if this person left your company - find them. At least there should be a company file identifying where, when, who etc. was involved last year. Why re-invent the wheel?

I'm sure if you looked at your past long-term assignments, you'd find they have some similarity to tasks done by co-workers. And yet, you start from scratch.

Before planning any long-term assignment, spend just five minutes trying to determine how you could be "lazy." In reality, you wouldn't be "lazy" but would be using effective time management. So, take five minutes before tackling assignments, to identify how you can "cut corners" or utilise work done in the past by yourself or others.

How to choose priorities:

Whether you plan your day the afternoon before or first thing in the morning, it's important to identify which tasks take priority.

Priority As - Important and Urgent, must be done right away.
Priority Bs - Important but *not* urgent, can be done now or later.

Priority Cs - Are often urgent to others but of low importance to you.

Priority Ds - Garbage - don't do these unimportant tasks.

Because you choose these priorities, it's only logical you should do them in the order of importance. When you set priorities this way, it keeps you from "getting off track" where you're tempted to do an easier task.

It pays to slot in tasks that have caused you difficulty because of procrastination into your highest energy level of the day.

Bring-Forward File:

Rather than sift through paperwork three or four times, it's handy to have a Bring-forward file (usually a pocket file with dates on each pocket). You use it to file information relating to tasks you want to tackle that particular day.

For instance, you have called to speak to George, only to find that he's out-of-town until Friday, the 6th. You would file the information with a note to remind you what you wanted to ask him under the 6th. This way you won't forget to get in touch with him that particular day.

The In Basket:

Every morning you probably face multiple e-mails and the "In Basket." This is how you can set priorities with all the information at hand:

For information that is actually in your desk in-basket:

1. Classify information into four piles - Priority As, Bs, Cs and Ds (I do the same with telephone messages and leftover assignments from the day before). Put Cs aside for later. Most of your Ds should be placed in "File 13" (your garbage can). Don't keep anything unless you really have a use for it. You could throw out 80 percent of your mail and not even miss it! As the day progresses and new assignments come along - do the same thing, slotting them

between two other tasks. Remember to check your BF (bring forward) file for that day.

2. Now that you have three piles - As, Bs and Cs (you've thrown out the Ds) determine whether you have enough time to complete your As. Do you have time to do any Bs as well? If so - add those to your list. If not - put these Bs in your bring forward file for later completion.

3. Find an empty folder and put all your Cs into it and put the file out of sight. Now you can deal exclusively with only the important and urgent items.

4. Next determine which is your Priority A1, A2, A3, A4, etc. and try to establish the time each task will take to complete.

5. **Clear your work area of all unnecessary items.**

6. Make a *To do* list of what you wish to accomplish that day. I make my *To do* list in pencil, so I can change a priority A5, to an A6 if necessary. Update this *To Do* list throughout the day as you slot in new assignments.

7. Remember to check your Daytimer or calendar for appointments and deadlines.

8. Know your limitations. If you find that you can't do all that's required that day – determine whether you should delegate any tasks to someone else or ask for help from your supervisor.

For information that comes in the form of e-mails:

1. On your computer e-mail service, make a file entitled "To Do." Then put sub-headings entitled As, Bs and Cs (delete the Ds).

2. Follow the same procedure you used for your desk information (the actual paperwork you deal with) and add the e-mail tasks to your *To Do* list.

Do you have trouble getting your Cs out of sight? They're easy and quick, but often cut into the time you should be spending on those important As. If this is the case - the following might help:

Reward vs. Punishment:

Behavioural science experts say that: *"Any behaviour that's followed by something pleasant is inclined to be re-enforced and is more likely to happen again. Punishing yourself for goofing-off is not nearly as effective as rewarding yourself for success."*

So, give yourself rewards (especially when particularly distasteful tasks are completed). This reward could be as simple as giving yourself an extended break after completing a difficult assignment or as elaborate as making arrangements to go to Hawaii.

Daytimers and "To Do" Lists:

1. To keep track of appointments and things you must do, do you use:
   Desk calendar?   Daytimer?   Other system?
2. Do you make "to do" lists every day - even on weekends?
3. How effective do you find the system you use to keep track of your time?

It's important for you to use whatever system works best for you. If you're satisfied with your system, the old adage, *"If it ain't broke - don't fix it."* applies.

I use both a daytimer and a "to do" list. When a company hires me to do a seminar, I write down everything I have to accomplish for their seminar on a separate "to do" list. I then put dates next to the tasks and transfer the information to my daytimer. Using this method, I seldom forget anything and have a back-up list that I can tick off when I complete the activities. My daytimer would have entries such as; when I sent a contract to a client; when it was signed and returned; did I send the workbooks; did I check to see that they had arrived; etc.

You can imagine what would happen if I forgot something so important as not telling a company that I required a

PowerPoint projector or forgetting to make travel arrangements until the last minute and finding seats were not available to allow me to arrive on time for the seminar? For me the dual "to do" system works well. What system would work for you? Once you decide, use it faithfully.

Solutions to Time Wasters:

Many problems in an office are caused by improper use of time by yourself or others. Here are some suggestions to common time management problems:

1. Telephone Interruptions:

    a) Differentiate between business and personal calls.
    b) Keep business calls to business matters.
    c) Set a time limit to conversations.
    d) When making phone calls - make a list of the issues you wish to discuss so you don't forget one of them and have to call back.

Many people encourage chatting. How you respond to someone who's showing signs that they want to chat, will determine the outcome of the conversation. For example: A regular client phones in and enquires, *"Hi Merle, did you have a nice long weekend?"* They can hook you with this kind of question and you'll probably spend the next fifteen minutes discussing your weekend. On the other hand, you could reply, *"It was great Merle, what can I do for you today?"* You've steered the conversation right back to the topic at hand. If you feel this is being too abrupt, you might say, *"It was great Merle. I wish I had time to tell you about it, but I'm swamped. What can I do for you today?"*

2. Drop-in Visitors:

    a) Distinguish business and personal visitors and treat accordingly.
    b) Have the receptionist screen visitors before they see you.

100

c) Discourage socialising - continue with your work. Be honest with visitors and state for instance: *"I've only got a few minutes - how can I help you."* Then stick to it.

3. Interruptions:

a) Keep a log to determine when, how long and who causes your interruptions. Determine how much of your day you spend dealing with interruptions. You may find that this is a large portion of your day so how you deal with those interruptions is important. If you feel as if others are keeping you from doing your "real" work, you may find yourself getting upset by the interruptions. This will make it difficult for you to get back to work. When you realise that interruptions are as much a part of your job as completing reports, your mental attitude should change towards these interruptions. Do this by telling yourself, *"That's my job calling."*

b) If the person wants to chat - suggest they catch you at coffee break.

c) Set time limits - and stick to them.

d) Meet others in their office - so you can leave when you wish. Or meet visitors in a conference room, reception area or in the hall if you want the meeting to be short.

If receptionists' desks are of average height, they might feel the need to chat with those waiting for appointments. Solve this problem by installing desks with a high front in the reception area. This allows staff to continue working, without having the guilty feeling that they're being rude to office visitors. This still allows them to see over the top of the barricade to check what visitors are doing and to monitor the waiting room.

4. Ineffective Delegation:

a) Talk with your manager to see if someone else can handle a duty that you feel doesn't fit your position.

b) Use paraphrasing to make sure you understand what your manager expects from you.

101

c) Ask for written instructions.

5. Meetings:

a) Be sure your attendance serves a purpose.
b) Is a meeting really necessary, or is it just a habit?
c) Come prepared for meetings with all necessary back-up information.

6. Lack of Objectives/Priorities and Planning:

a) Ask for an up-to-date job description that includes standards of performance.
b) Define priority items.
c) Make 'to do' lists and follow them.

7. Dealing with Crisis Situations:

a) Assess how often it happens.
b) Determine how future crisis can be stopped (preventive maintenance).
c) Allow time for "fighting fires" every day.
d) Don't put off or procrastinate (which can start a crisis.)

8. Attempting Too Much at Once:

a) Set objectives and priorities.
b) Make daily "to do" lists.
c) Know how and when to say *"No"* to additional duties.

9. Cluttered Desk/Personal Disorganisation:

a) Allow time to organise - it will save time later.
b) Minimise paperwork.
c) Use verbal communication as often as possible.
d) Put away anything that you're not working on at present.
e) Everything has a place.

10. Inability to Say "No:"

a) Take an assertiveness training course.
b) Know that you can't please all the people all the time.

c) Recognise traps, manipulative games that can "con" you into doing things you don't want to.

d) Offer alternative solutions.

e) Decide the consequences should you say, *"Yes."*

f) Every *"No"* does not have to be explained to others.

g) Count to ten before saying, *"Yes."*

h) Better to do less well, than more poorly.

11. Unclear Communication/Instruction:

a) Develop listening skills.

b) Practice paraphrasing and feedback.

c) Repeat instructions.

12. Confused Responsibility & Authority:

a) Have up-to-date job description.

b) Determine your level of responsibility and make sure you have the authority to carry out your responsibilities.

c) Determine your subordinates' level of responsibility and authority.

13. Delayed, Inaccurate Information:

a) Check your information source - don't listen to the company grapevine.

b) Identify and deal with bottleneck employees.

c) Practice listening skills.

d) Use paraphrasing and feedback.

e) Speak, don't write - except to back up information.

14. Lack of Self-Discipline:

a) Keep a daily "to do" list.

b) Set objectives and plan daily.

c) Set priorities and stick to them.

d) Schedule unpleasant tasks first.

15. Leaving Tasks Unfinished: Same as #14

16. Untrained, Inadequate Staff:

a) Use "old Timers" in your department for training of your staff.

b) Ask for training where you or your staff need it.

c) Know where company policy manuals are kept and read them.

d) Keep your own information file of things you've learned - keep for future use.

17. Socialising:

a) Control the urge to socialise unnecessarily.

b) Keep your own socialising to coffee and lunch breaks.

c) Keep busy!

18. Indecision/Procrastination:

a) Take an assertiveness training course.

b) Daily "to do" lists keeps you on track.

c) Ask others to help you determine when you're being indecisive or showing procrastination.

d) Have faith that you have the ability to do the job.

How to manage interruptions:

Interruptions are a normal part of your day. Most people don't allow enough time to look after them, therefore become stressed-out by the end of the day. Try the following - see if things change:

1. Set a time limit - and stick to it. Say *"I don't have a minute - but I do have five."* Start timing.

2. Set the stage in advance - you're truly busy!

3. Tell your phone caller about your A1 priority.

4. Keep a pencil in your hand.

5. Keep your hands on the keyboard.

6. With drop-ins, stay standing. If they sit - you sit on the desk.

7. Meet them in their office, so you can leave when you want to.

8. Meet visitors in a conference room or reception area - or in the hall if you want the meeting to be short.
9. Avoid small talk when busy - makes large interruptions out of small ones.
10. Try not to feel annoyed when interrupted.
11. Give interrupters undivided attention. Listen carefully.
12. Don't interrupt others.
13. Don't let your mind drift - it's time-consuming.
14. Get them to the point. You might ask, *"What is your problem with this?"* or *"What is the main purpose of this meeting?"* Say, *"No."* if they ask for too much.

On the other hand:

15. Don't let them go away empty handed. Promise to do it later. Explain that you're working on other priorities. Tell them who else they might call.
16. Other things to say to keep it short: *"Could we continue this, when I'm not so swamped?"* Or on the phone *"I've got that down and will be back to you soon."*
17. Or: Glance at the clock a few times. Tell them you have another appointment now. Stand up - hold out your hand and ease them towards the door.

Get back on track after interruptions. Don't use interruptions as excuses to procrastinate. Don't complain or take a break after interruptions.

How to prevent interruptions:

1. Re-organise your work area. Be less accessible. Move your desk so you are not seen as people walk along the hallway.
2.   Don't have too many chairs near your desk.
3. Have a clock in a prominent place.
4. Drown out exterior noise, wear earplugs if necessary.
5. Turn down the volume on your phone bell or install an on/off switch on your phone.

6. Use "Do Not Disturb" sign for your door or any other humorous message when necessary.
7. An "Open door policy" can be a time killer unless you keep to business matters.
8. Remove yourself - go to a conference room or library (as a last resort lock yourself in the bathroom).
9. Ask your personal assistant to take calls and screen visitors - decide beforehand that calls you wish to accept.
10. Tell people what you're doing.

More Ways to Prevent Interruptions:

1. Hold calls for two hours a day so you can work on your A1.
2. Only accept calls or visitors during announced hours.
3. Keep a visitor and telephone interruption log. Study it. Spot the interruptions on your staff. Meet with them and discuss the problem. Delegate projects that cause interruptions for you.
4. Encourage weekly staff meetings - keep everyone current.
5. Have regular morning meetings with your assistant - go over both your "to do" lists.
6. Ask staff interrupters to write down their problem and list possible solutions.

Are you at fault? Do you:

1. Panic if your phone doesn't ring?
2. Take unnecessary trips to get coffee or water?
3. Start a project before you finish the first one?
4. Pass on gossip.
5. Tell people personal problems and then you have to listen to theirs?
6. Eavesdrop or encourage dropper-inners?
7. Keep people too long at meetings?
8. Friends and family call too often or you call them too often?

How to Control Crisis:

A. Some Don'ts:

- Don't become unglued or lose your cool. It makes things worse and can make enemies.
- Be more concerned about what people will think of you than coping with the problem.
- Throw good time management out the window.

B. Some Dos:

1. Use your energy towards finding solutions - not for yelling or fuming.
2. Think about the problem, not your performance.
3. Take a moment to consider your options.
4. Try to relax before tackling the problem - prepare mentally.
5. Continue delegating what you can.
6. Prepare a plan of action.
7. Take crisis in stride as just part of a normal day.

C. Turn a Crisis into an Opportunity

Try new methods, shortcuts and better procedures.

D. Reduce Crisis:

1. Practice good time management with "to do" lists, A, B, C and D priorities. Don't procrastinate.
2. Anticipate known deadlines! Don't put assignments off till the last minute.
3. Check weekly or monthly with staff. Are any personality conflicts brewing?
4. Check with your boss. Can you improve your performance?
5. Make contingency plans, cross train and anticipate crisis.

Assistants' suggestions for bosses:

Keep us informed (communicate). Tell us:

- What you expect;
- How we're doing;

- What's behind the e-mail;
- Why things are important;
- Where you're going and when you'll be back.
- Let us make some decisions (confidence) especially with routine matters when we know the answer. We'll gain confidence, feel more important and as if we're part of the team.
- Keep our work flowing (consideration).
- Prepare before giving us instructions (consideration) don't fumble through papers, mumble into your fist or change it all with an afterthought.
- When you make appointments - keep them (consideration). Save us the embarrassment of having to deal with angry visitors.
- When others have requested you to give information or make decisions, get back to them promptly (consideration) otherwise we're left to explain.

Working With Your Personal Assistant:

Here are some suggestions to bosses that show how their personal assistants can help them more. One of the most important things you can do is:

1. When delegating work to your staff, use coloured labels - for instance: Red for Urgent (require immediate attention); Yellow (do today) and Green (can wait until tomorrow). Make sure a date is put on the information. Do the same for e-mail assignments. This saves your staff from wasting time trying to determine priorities.
2. Your assistant must be able to see you early in the day so s/he can help you plan both your days.
3. Have your assistant answer routine letters and e-mails for you.
4. Set aside time in the early part of the day and afternoon as your uninterrupted time. Have your assistant take messages during this time - only take emergency calls.

5. Give your assistant the authority to screen your calls - make sure it's known who is important, and what people you wish to speak to.

6. Give your assistant the authority to sign your routine letters, leaving only critical, sensitive or legal letters for your attention.

7. Have magazines etc. routed to others in your department. Readers circle any interesting article in the Table of Contents. When the magazine is returned, you'll already know which articles are worth reading.

8. When awaiting information - put existing information in your bring forward file to keep them available - but not in the way.

9. Make sure your assistant is aware of any deadlines you have. Obtain his/her help in meeting those deadlines - by making sure files are ready, getting information for you, etc.

10. If you share an assistant, make sure you and the other supervisors keep in touch. Have an early morning meeting with them. Instruct your assistant to let you know if there is too much to do and help choose priorities by discussing work with the other supervisors.

11. Meeting notes should include lists of people responsible for carrying out a task, the decisions made and any deadlines. Keep track of completed assignments. At the next meeting put those that have not been completed under "unfinished business."

12. Make sure your assistant has an up-to-date position description that includes all areas of responsibility. Make sure you've given him/her the authority to carry out these duties and explained the accountability to you for the completion of the tasks. A maximum of 10 percent should be allotted to "other duties as assigned."

13. Your position description as a supervisor includes consideration, confidence, and communication with your assistant.

14. Your effectiveness depends as much on your assistant's abilities as yours. Assistants often benefit from training so they can understand your role more fully.
15. Help organise each other.
16. Get along by putting up with each other's differences.
17. Supervisors and assistants make up their own "to do" lists and then agree on priorities.
18. Make sure your assistant knows where you are.
19. Pay your assistant what s/he's worth. An effective assistant doubles the effectiveness of a boss - while a poor one cuts productivity in half. Pay what it takes to get and keep the best.

Procrastination:

A serious time problem is procrastination that can cause serious problems in the workplace. It's a major cause for termination of employees.

See if you can determine times when procrastination is a problem with you. What kinds of tasks stimulate this procrastination? How can you tell when procrastination has become a serious problem? When you:

- Have something important to do, not much time to do it in, but find yourself looking for other things to do instead.
- Set deadlines, but don't meet them.
- Constantly delay making important decisions.
- Work furiously at the last minute to complete crucial assignments.

Five Types of Procrastinators:

1. **Last-minute type** - They wait until the last minute and work around the clock to meet deadlines.
2. **I'll make a decision later** - They postpone decisions until events resolve the situation or they're forced to make a decision.

3. **Perfectionists** - They must complete all tasks faultlessly, no matter how small. They need to learn to discriminate in the importance they place on assignments.
4. **I'll show you!** - They delay assignments as a way of retaining a sense of personal power and control. (Watch for this sign in your staff. They may use to "get back" at you when assigned distasteful duties).
5. **Muddler** - They put off work because of bad habits, poor organisation, trying to do too much or lack of set procedures. They're the people who go around in ever widening circles - getting nowhere. They start an assignment and before completing it, start another one and very seldom complete assignments on time.

Lateness:

There are three basic kinds of personalities when it comes to time usage. Let's assume there was a meeting called for 10:00 am:

Type A: This person would arrive right at 10:00 am.

Type B: This person would arrive at 10:10 am and feel they were on time.

Type C: This person would arrive at 9:50 and feel that they *"just made it!"*

Those who arrive ten minutes late run into more problems than the early bird. What do you think runs through the minds of those who cared enough to be there on time? Those waiting probably feel that the latecomer thinks they aren't important. Otherwise, why would they act as if their time was more important than those waiting? This is a serious put-down that causes hidden repercussions later for the latecomer.

The person who is ten minutes early, can waste that time (waiting time) or s/he can be smart and bring some short-term task s/he can complete in the ten minutes.

Summary:

- Learn to consider that waiting time is a "gift of time" and use it wisely.
- Make a daily "to do" list to be certain that you're moving steadily toward your goals, not just filling hours.
- Instead of listing tasks on scraps of paper - have one list.
- Rewrite (or update) your list as new items come up during the day.
- Start with A's not C's.
- Set priorities and do your A-1 right now.
- Remember - it's not crossing out items that counts; but making better use of your time.
- Don't schedule every minute of the day with appointments. Save some uncommitted time.
- Use the "Swiss Cheese" approach for long-term complex tasks by identifying instant tasks.
- Select the best time of the day for the type of work to be completed.
- Keep a time log and record how you actually spend your time.
- Before you start something, consider delegating it.
- Learn to say *"no"* graciously. Recognise that it's better to say *"no"* at the start than disappoint people because you've over- committed.
- Ask yourself, *"Is this meeting really necessary?*
- Clearly identify the purpose and objectives of a meeting.
- Prepare a written agenda and distribute it in advance to give attendees time to prepare for meetings.
- Stick to the agenda.
- Consider time as money - and invest it wisely.
- Try increasing your work pace from time to time.
- Improve your follow-up on delegated tasks.
- Spend more time training subordinates to do a better job.
- Avoid the tendency to *"Do it yourself."*

112

- Never put off until tomorrow - what you can get someone else to do today.
- Meet visitors in the reception area rather than your office.
- Try to concentrate on only one thing at a time; learn to focus.
- Keep a reminder of your top priority tasks in a place you will notice after handling an interruption.
- Set deadlines for yourself (and others).
- If possible, answer letters and enquiries by phone right now.
- Throw out 20 percent of your mail. You'll never miss it.
- Cancel unnecessary subscriptions Get everyone on your team thinking about better time management by asking, *"What can I do to help you make better use of your time?"*

How much time do we have?

Have you ever sat down and considered how much time you have to do all the things you want to do in your lifetime?

Today, in first world countries, women's average lifespan is 84 years and rising. Men's is 79 years and rising. The gap between men and women's lifespan is decreasing because of two major reasons. Women are making more decisions that result in raised stress level. Because women are sharing this task, men's stress levels are lower. Women are quitting smoking at a slower rate than men.

In this new century, most people can look forward to being alive, well into their 80s and 90s. You can see our lifespan is increasing rapidly. In the next twenty years, half the population in developed countries will be 65 years of age or older. This should convince you to take care of your body. By correcting eating or drinking habits, by exercising and quitting smoking you'll probably enjoy those extra years much more.

So, how much time do we have?

- 24 hours in a day;

- 1440 minutes in a day;
- 168 hours in a week;
- 8,760 hours in a year;
- 657,000 hours in 75 years;
- 27,375 days in 75 years.

I've shown total hours and days for a lifespan of 75 years. At the beginning of the 1900's, man's life expectancy was 43. This meant that if you were 22 years of age, you were middle-aged!

Time breakdown hours/week

What does the average person do with their 168 hours in a week?

- Sleep: 56
- Personal hygiene: 7
- Eating: 7
- Travel: 5.25
- Work: 66.5
- Pleasure: 9
- Self improvement: 1.75
- Illness: 1.5
- Total: 150 hours
- Hours unaccounted for: 18

The above survey shows that the average person sleeps 8 hours a night. How many hours do you sleep per night? Is this through choice or necessity? Do you need less or more than average?

If you said you need more sleep, could it be because life is so boring you regularly choose sleeping as a way of spending your time? Do you find that you don't seem to have anything worthwhile to get up for? If this is the case, get more challenge in your life.

Personal Hygiene: is bathing, shaving, putting on makeup, combing your hair etc.

Eating: is just the time it takes to eat, not the socialising that goes along with it.

Travel: includes travelling to work, doing grocery shopping, errands and driving the kids to their soccer game.

Work: includes paid and unpaid work. Women's weekly totals are normally much higher than men's. Most men work for 45 years of their adult lives before retirement. Women work an average of 35 years of their adult lives (either part-time or full-time) in paid employment (plus home and childcare) before retirement.

Pleasure: includes watching TV, reading a novel, participating or watching sports, going to a party, etc. This is the area of your life where you let your "little kid" out.

Self-improvement: includes all the time you spent at regular school as well as any courses you've attended since then. This includes reading non-fiction books, obtaining in-house training etc.

Illness: (self explanatory)

What are we doing with the 18 hours that are unaccounted for? It's spent waiting for something or someone or just goofing-off (necessary under some conditions).

How do you spend your time? You may find surprises when you complete the following sheet for one week. Possibly you're spending more time watching TV than you thought you were. You might decide to spend that time more constructively towards reaching your goals.

Time Breakdown:

There are 168 hours in a week. How did you spend your time within this past week? Make a graph with the following headings: Activity: Sunday; Monday; Tuesday etc. Under Activity put:

- Sleep
- Personal Hygiene (washing, hair care, makeup, shaving)
- Eating
- Travel (commuting)
- Work (salaried)
- Work (home)
- Pleasure (TV, sports, reading)
- Self Development (education, study)
- Illness
- Total

Then, decide how much time you spend at or with:

a) Working
b) Family
c) Social (community)
d) Goof-off time or illness

Inevitably, there will be days when you'll end up frustrated, with commitments stretching endlessly before you. Don't be ashamed to admit when you're in over your head. Perhaps you can delegate several of your responsibilities to another employee (at least temporarily). If you find you're constantly working overtime, it's either:

1. You have too many responsibilities or
2. You're not using effective time management.

Now that you have your time problems under control, it's time to attack your interpersonal or communication skills.

CHAPTER SIX

INTERPERSONAL SKILLS

When we speak of interpersonal skills - what do we mean? What skills does this involve?

- Speaking;
- Listening;
- Writing;
- Reading;
- Non-verbal communication (body language);
- Understanding others (empathy); and
- Reacting to the behaviour of others.

If you're often misunderstood or others constantly misinterpret what you say or write, there are several skills that can correct these problems:

How to Listen:

When you think of it, most of us never received instructions on how to listen. We assume that because we've been listening since infancy that we must be doing it right. Not so! Most of us as children were taught how to "be quiet" - not how to listen.

Our metabolism is our own worst enemy when it comes to listening. Here are some facts that surprised me when I did my research on this topic:

- We listen in spurts. Most of us are unable to give hard, close attention to what's being said for more than 60 seconds at a time. We concentrate – we let up - then we concentrate again.
- We spend about 80 percent of our waking hours using our four basic communication skills, speaking, listening writing and reading. We spend half of that time doing

nothing but listening (this is 40 percent of our waking hours).

How fast do you think people normally speak in words per minute? How about thinking? How fast are we able to think in words per minute?

I've had speaking speed guesstimates of from 60 to 200 words per minute. The average person speaks about 125 to 150 words per minute.

When I do my seminars, I speak at about 160 words per minute. Radio announcers speak at 180 words per minute and auctioneers - who's counted?

Most people would guess that people are capable of thinking from 75 to 150 words per minute. This is where the surprise occurs. People are normally able to think at anywhere from 750 to 1,200 words per minute! So, what happens if I'm talking at my normal rate of speaking (160 w.p.m.)? The listener's brain becomes bored, so it goes off on side-trips such as:

- *"Jim sure needs to go on a diet."*
- *"I wonder where she got that idea?"*
- *"I wonder why Sally changed her hairstyle?"*
- *"I wonder how long it is till coffee break?"*
- *"Why was Bob so mad at me this morning?"*
- *"I know an example of that."*
- *"What should we have for dinner tonight?"*

Because listeners can listen so much faster than the speaker can talk, they tend to waver in their attention. Unfortunately, during this lapse they miss important information. For example, did you turn the radio on this morning so you could catch the time or the weather report? Did you hear the message when the announcer gave it or had you "tuned" him out?

A hundred years ago, if you heard a voice, you knew that voice was probably talking to you - not some machine that you could tune out mentally. This tune-out ability is crucial in most noisy office or work situations. If we couldn't, the surrounding distractions would cause concentration difficulties. But it does make us terrible listeners because of it.

Good listeners learn to identify when they've tuned out. They bring themselves back into the conversation before they lose important information. The next time you're talking with someone or listening to someone speak on television or radio, see if you can identify when you "tune-out." The more you catch yourself, the better you'll be at tuning back in. If you don't catch yourself, you're either an exceptionally good listener, the speaker kept your attention, or you didn't identify when you *did* tune-out.

Blocks to effective listening:

Besides tune-outs, there are many other things that can cause us to miss vital information. Do the following hamper you from being a good listener?

1. You had trouble understanding the speaker's words.
2. You were thinking of what you were going to say when the speaker was talking.
3. You know you have prejudices, but s/he really tested them.
4. You didn't have enough knowledge to grasp the message.
5. You listened for what you wanted to hear.
6. You were too tired mentally to work at paying attention.
7. There were outside noises and distractions.
8. The speaker had poor delivery; slow, windy, irrelevant, rambling or repetitious.
9. Something the speaker said intrigued you – you thought about it - and when you came back to the conversation, you'd lost the thread of it.
10. The speaker was a "know-it-all."
11. The speaker had an accent and you had difficulty understanding him/her. Your brain tuned out after a while

because you had to work too hard to catch the meaning of the speaker's words.

12. You were too far ahead of the speaker by trying to understand things too soon.
13. You forgot to use paraphrasing and feedback to listen effectively.
14. You felt you were being given far too much information.
15. The person seemed to talk down to you.

How do you rate as a listener?

Rate yourself (or have a friend help you) using the following scale:

5= Always
4= Almost always
3= Sometimes
2= Rarely
1= Never

1. I allow the speaker to express his or her complete thoughts without interrupting.
2. I actively try to develop my ability to remember important facts.
3. In a conference or important phone conversation, I write down the most important details of a message.
4. I avoid becoming hostile or excited if a speaker's views differ from mine.
5. I repeat the essential details of a conversation back to the speaker to confirm that I have understood correctly.
6. I exercise tact in keeping the speaker on track.
7. I tune out distractions when listening.
8. I make an effort to show interest in the other person's conversation.
9. I understand that I'm learning little when I'm talking. (I talk too much, listen too little?)
10. I sound as if I'm listening. (I use paraphrasing, ask questions.)

11. I remember that people are less defensive when they feel they're being understood.
12. I understand that I don't have to agree with the speaker.
13. In personal conversation, I look for non-verbal forms of communication, such as body language, tone of voice and other signals that provide information in addition to the speaker's words.
14. I look as if I'm listening in personal meetings. (I lean forward, give eye contact.)
15. I ask for the spelling of names and places when I'm taking a message.

TOTAL:

Scoring:

- 64 or more - You're an excellent listener!
- 50 - 63 - You're better than average.
- 40 - 49 - You require improvement.
- 39 or less - You're not an effective listener. You need practice, practice and more practice!

Regarding questions #5 and 6: remember everyone's entitled to their own opinion. You don't have to agree with them all the time. If you were discussing a controversial topic (such as abortion or capital punishment) it's possible you may be on opposite sides of the issue. If you find your discussion is going nowhere or you're both becoming angry or defensive, don't let the situation continue. Instead, make the comment, *"You're entitled to your opinion, and I'm entitled to my opinion. Let's agree to disagree and not discuss it any more."*

Caution: Save these comments only for those subjects that display distinct differences of opinions and neither person will sway in their position.

For question #6: When a person gets off topic, use paraphrasing say, *"I want to make sure I've got the information*

I need." Or you might say, *"We're getting a little off topic here. We were discussing ..."*

With question #15: whenever you're taking down someone's name, ask the person how to spell it (even the name Smith may be spelled Smythe). In brackets (below the spelling of the name) add your own phonetic pronunciation of the name. For instance, the last name GIESBRECHT would be phonetically (Geez-beckt); CARPHIN--(Car-fin); CEBULIAK--(Ceb-u-luck), etc.

This technique is very helpful to the person who may be returning the call. I use it on client files, so I pronounce the person's name properly when I contact them. Here's how you can:

Improve your listening skills:

1. You must care enough to want to improve. Without this motivation, it'll be too much effort.
2. Try to find an uninterrupted area in which to converse. Keeping your train of thought is difficult when there are obstructions to concentration.
3. Try to talk about matters that are of known interest to the other person. Try to find their "hot button."
4. Try not to anticipate what the other person will say.
5. Be mindful of your own biases and prejudices, so they don't unduly influence your listening.
6. Pay careful attention to what's being said without planning rebuttals to it.
7. Be aware of "red flag words" which trigger over-reaction. Examples of this are, "women's libber," or "male chauvinist."
8. Don't allow yourself to get too far ahead of the speaker by trying to understand things too soon.
9. At intervals, try to paraphrase what people have been saying to clarify the meaning of the conversation.

10. When you have difficulty determining the reasoning behind a conversation, ask, *"Why are you telling me this?"*
11. Watch for key or buzz words if you find you've lost the train of the conversation. This usually happens when listening to long-winded people or those who ramble.
12. Analytical people have a difficult time in conversation. Their personal need to know every detail might make the person in the conversation feel as if they're being grilled.

Qualities of a good listener:

People who practice good listening skills do the following:

1. Let others finish what they're saying (don't interrupt others).
2. If they don't follow the line of conversation, they ask questions.
3. They keep comfortable eye contact - don't let their eyes wander around the room.
4. Pay attention to what others are saying.
5. Remain open-minded - ready to change their opinion.
6. Use feedback and paraphrasing skills.
7. Read others' non-verbal or body language well.
8. Don't "tune out" inappropriately when others are speaking.

Another communication skill is the art of being able to say what you want to say. Verbal fluency enables you to express your thoughts clearly, so others understand exactly what you mean. Here's a test you can give yourself. As we often don't see ourselves clearly, it might be a helpful to have a friend do it for you as well.

How do you rate as a Speaker?

Rate yourself (or have a friend help you) using the following scale:

5= Always
4= Almost always

123

3= Sometimes
2= Rarely
1= Never

1. If I were a listener, would I listen to myself?
2. If I'm being misunderstood, I remember that it's my responsibility to help the other person understand me.
3. I keep my instructions to others short, sweet and to the point.
4. I am aware of when my audience has tuned me out.
5. I make sure my listeners know what I want from them.
6. When I give instructions, I ask for feedback and paraphrasing to make sure I'm understood.
7. I make sure my non-verbal signals (body language, tone of voice, etc.) are the same as my verbal ones.
8. I make sure I don't intimidate my listeners with a loud voice, threatening appearance, intense or prolonged eye contact, verbal attacks, etc.
9. I articulate clearly. Don't mumble.
10. I try to use language the listener can understand.

TOTAL:

Scoring:

- 40 or more - You're an excellent speaker!
- 32 - 39 - You're better than average.
- 25 - 31 - You require improvement.
- 24 or less- You're not an effective speaker. You need practice, practice and more practice!

Did you chuckle to yourself when completing the first question? Did you find there was an element of truth in the question? It's possible that you fit into one of three categories of people who believe they're not worth listening to:

a) Have trouble getting the words out. They know what they want to say but can't quite say it (lack verbal fluency).

Because you're going to be talking the rest of your life, it certainly seems worthwhile to improve this essential communication skill. As a supervisor, this is even more important. Join Toastmasters or Toastmistress clubs or take a public speaking course.

b) Not up on what's going on. Often people insulate themselves from the terrible things that are going on in the world. Suddenly, in social situations they may find they don't know what's going on, therefore feel they have nothing to contribute to the conversation. The solution is to catch up on what's happening.

c) It's possible that you "run off at the mouth," have problems keeping conversations short, sweet and to the point. Spend some time organising your thoughts before you speak. Practice by writing down your thoughts or use a tape recorder to catch yourself. Then re-word your conversation using more precise language.

If question three is a problem, (c) will help here as well. Use the KISS principle:

Keep it simple sweetie - or
Keep it simple stupid (depending on how you feel at the time).

In question 5, if you want something from someone or want their opinion, ask them for their help before you give them the background information. For example:

A man came home from work and wanted to discuss a work problem with his wife. She had put in a rather tiring day herself. He gave her all kinds of details on what was happening and surprised her out of half-listening by asking, *"What do you think I should do?"*

She felt embarrassed because she had not been paying attention. He had to repeat the entire commentary again. It would have been better if he had started the conversation, *"Mary, I need your opinion on something that's happening at*

125

the office. Do you have time to discuss it right now?" Then he would have confirmed that she did have time, as well as receive her undivided attention.

Communication tips:

Here are a few common-sense guidelines to make sure you won't be misunderstood:

- Start with clear thinking. Sort out what you want to say.
- Pause to collect your thoughts before you speak. In a one-on-one conversation, don't feel you have to jump right in with a response the second the other person finishes speaking.
- Sort out what you want to say. This lets the other person know that you're taking time to digest what s/he has said. If you jump right in, the moment the other person stops talking or interrupt - it's probably an indication to him/her that you haven't been listening.
- Choose your words carefully.
- Watch for non-verbal signs of agreement or disagreement.
- Don't use big words to impress your listener. Try to avoid words that have double meanings. Remember that words don't carry the same meaning from one part of the country to the next. You have to put yourself in the other person's place. Try to understand his/her point of view and what s/he brings to the conversation or discussion.
- In face-to-face conversation, much of what we communicate is non-verbal, so learn how to read the signals correctly. Sometimes the person will nod absent-mindedly, as if s/he is agreeing with you. However, s/he may not agree with you at all. S/he may even be thinking about something entirely different from the subject you're discussing.
- Other non-verbal signs - a smile, a frown, a questioning look, a fidgeting listener - give you signals on whether or

not you're being understood. Don't overlook these non-verbal signs, but don't put too much emphasis on them either. Watch their eyes. Eye contact is important in communicating effectively.

Be a good listener:

You can't effectively respond to what the other person saying if you allow yourself to get distracted. You're not listening if you're deciding where to go for dinner or trying to analyse why your spouse was cranky that morning.

To be a good listener, you have to concentrate - and concentration requires discipline. Clear your mind of other thoughts and problems: give the other person your full attention. Look the speaker in the eye, rather than letting yourself glance around the room at things that may distract you.

Speak clearly and distinctly. Watch your diction. Do you mumble or run your words together? Remember who you're speaking to and their conversation level.

More than one misunderstanding has occurred because the listener didn't hear your words the same way you said them. This is especially important if you have an accent or if you're speaking with people whose native language is not the same as yours. Try to use well-known English words.

Writing skills:

Most of these same basic guidelines apply to the written word, except you don't have any way to watch the other person's reaction. In writing, it's even more critical that you organise your thoughts, choose your words carefully and present your message in a way it can't be misunderstood.

Write as if you were talking with the receiver. Remember that you won't be able to say, *"But that isn't what I meant!"* when the other person is reading your letter, e-mail or report. Be sure that your words aren't taken the wrong way by the receiver.

Encourage your assistant to identify anything in your correspondence that isn't clear, so this type of misunderstanding doesn't occur.

Message loss through repetition:

Do you remember the game you played in primary school? A message was given to one child. This message was passed one by one to all the students. The original and final messages are compared, and discrepancies identified.

The following information is crucial to those involved in training. If I train Mary how to do something and she trains June, who trains Sam; do you think Sam would receive the same training I gave Mary? Here are the normal changes that occur in the passing of information:

       1st speaker: 100% correct
       2nd speaker: 60%
       3rd speaker: 40%
       4th speaker: 20%
       5th speaker: 10%

When you're the recipient of a rumour or gossip, you can see the same thing could happen. Always go to the source of information and check it out. I can guarantee there have been changes along the way that have altered the meaning.

For example: A company had gone through a tough time financially but had received such a huge contract that they decided that they needed to move to a larger facility to fulfil the order. They told their employees that there would be a meeting at 4:00 pm on Wednesday.

On Monday morning a man wearing a tool belt came to the front desk and told the receptionist that he was there to measure the rooms. She asked why and he said it was for the new owners.

Well, you can imagine the conclusion the receptionist came to by hearing this information. By Tuesday afternoon, half the people in the company were actively looking for work elsewhere. The management learned about this and moved the meeting up to Tuesday afternoon to give them the good news.

So, do check out rumours and don't make the mistake of assuming what you are hearing means something it does not.

Communication process

Here are the eight steps in the communication process:

1. What I want to say.
2. What I actually say.
3. What the other person hears.
4. What the person thinks s/he hears.
5. What the person wants to respond.
6. What the person actually responds.
7. What I hear person say.
8. What I think I hear the person say.

How to avoid being misunderstood:

There are many ways we can be misunderstood. See how you rate yourself in the following. Make four headings:

What could I improve?
Need to do it less:
Doing all right:
Need to do more:

Expressing information, ideas, suggestions

1. Being brief, concise and getting to the point.
2. Being definite rather than hesitant and apologetic.
3. Talking in specifics, giving examples and details.
4. Talking in generalisations.

Expressing feelings

Letting others know when:

1. I don't understand something they've said.
2. I like something they've said or done.
3. I disagree with them.
4. I feel they've changed the subject or have become irrelevant.
5. I'm getting irritated.
6. I feel hurt or embarrassed.

Understanding information, ideas and suggestions of others

1. Listening to understand, rather than to prepare my next remark.
2. Helping others to participate in the discussion.
3. Before agreeing or disagreeing, check to make sure I understand what others mean.
4. Summarising points of disagreement.
5. Asking questions in ways that get more information than *"yes"* or *"no."*

Understanding and responding to others' feelings:

1. Checking out what I think others are feeling, rather than assuming I know.
2. Responding to a person who's angry with me, so I don't ignore his/her feelings.
3. Responding to a person whose feelings are hurt in a way that I don't ignore his/her feelings.
4. Responding to a person who's expressing closeness and affection for me in a way that I don't ignore his/her feelings.
5. Surveying a group to determine how much agreement exists (making group decisions).

General:

1. Talking in group discussions.
2. Getting feedback, encouraging others to let me know how my actions affect them.

3. Being aware when I'm trying to cope with my own feelings of discomfort rather than responding to the other persons.
4. Accepting help from others.
5. Offering help to others.
6. Yielding to others, giving in to others.
7. Standing up for myself.
8. Feel free to express my ideas.
9. Being empathetic towards others.
10. Reading non-verbal messages.
11. Frustration when dealing with difficult situations.
12. Ability to handle my own anger.

How did you rate? Put a * next to any that you've itemised as "Need to do less" or "Need to do more." Set some goals to improve your rating.

Surveys show that expressing information, ideas and suggestions is more of a problem for women. Although women have larger vocabularies than most men, they neglect to use "logic" in their conversation (which is what the men are looking for). For example: Women will often say *"I think ..."* *"I feel ..."* and *"I believe ..."* These preambles are okay in conversation, providing she follows up by including facts on why she thinks, feels or believes something is true.

On the other hand, "Expressing feelings" is more of a problem for men as described in the feedback section. Because many men aren't aware of what they're really feeling, they can't seem to talk about it or will say, *"I don't want to talk about it!"*

Another example: A boss feels disappointed because he lost a big sale. He enters his office and slams the door. His reaction demonstrates anger - not his feelings of disappointment. His staff probably misinterpret his behaviour and wonder what they did wrong.

It would have been much better if the boss had reacted as he felt. He would have explained his disappointment in the loss of the sale to his staff. This would have removed anxiety in his staff and given them a clearer message about his feelings.

Skill of Paraphrasing:

One valuable communication technique is the skill of paraphrasing. It will save countless misunderstandings and will clear up all those "grey areas" that crop up in conversation. Paraphrasing deals with words. It:

- Expresses meaning in other words;
- Is a re-statement of text or words;
- Gives the meaning another form; and/or
- Amplifies a message.

We normally use paraphrasing for simple things such as, repeating telephone numbers when taking a message. But how often do you transpose two numbers in taking down seven or eight simple digits of a phone number? The use of paraphrasing is essential when two people are conversing at any time. Unfortunately, when information isn't clear, we often make assumptions. We don't confirm with the other person that what we thought they said was what they really meant us to understand.

Has anyone ever given you instructions on how to get to their home and you neglected to use paraphrasing? Did you forget to make sure you understood their directions and ended up completely lost?

Here's an example of two people talking but not fully understanding each other:

> Bill: *"Jim didn't get that job he wanted."*
> Jennie: *"He didn't get the job he wanted?"*
> Bill: *"No and he's really upset about it."*

132

In this conversation, Jennie thought she was using paraphrasing, but all she was doing was parroting what Bill said. Instead, she should have asked herself what Bill's statement meant to her. Some of her assumptions could have been:

- Jim may have asked for too much money.
- He was overqualified for the position.
- He was under-qualified for the position.
- He blew the interview.
- Someone else was better than he.
- He's probably better suited to a different career.

After determining what the statement meant to her, (Jim blew the interview) and using paraphrasing, the earlier conversation would have been more like:

> Bill: *"Jim didn't get that job he wanted."*
> Jennie: *"You mean he blew the interview?"*
> Bill: *"Oh no, he learned that they had already chosen someone else for the position before he applied."*

You can see the differences between these two sets of conversations. In the first conversation, Bill and Jennie didn't clarify their personal beliefs with each other. Bill obviously misunderstood Jennie's message that he confirmed with his second conversation. He thinks Jennie knows Jim didn't get the job because the company had already chosen someone else.

Jennie on the other hand, believes that Bill has confirmed her belief that Jim blew the interview. This is why problems occurred later.

In a conversation with another friend, Jennie stated that both she and Bill agreed that Jim had blown the interview. She honestly believed that she was speaking the truth to her friend.

This kind of problem exists in most conversations, so ask for more information if you're not sure what a person means or use paraphrasing to bring out discrepancies. You probably use this technique already. If you have ever exclaimed, *"No that's not*

133

what I meant" - you've already used paraphrasing. Use it often: it lessens communication problems.

It's also an excellent tool to use when clients are angry at something. If you write down details of the situation you're trying to correct, you're less likely to be spending your energy defending yourself. When they've given all the information you need to solve the problem, use paraphrasing to make sure they know you *do* understand. Your client will likely calm down and give you the opportunity to help them.

Use paraphrasing to lock-in training of another. If they're lazy listeners, they'll improve immeasurably when they understand that your training methods include a "test." This test would go as follows: *"Sandy, this is what I want you to do. This is step one ... step two ... step three."*

You would then ask her to repeat back to you. Don't simply ask, *"Did you understand?"*

Some find they "get their back up" by the way others use paraphrasing. In this case, the person asking for paraphrasing probably gave the listener the impression they "were too dumb" to pick up the information.

The speaker (or giver of information) must understand that the onus is on them to make sure they were clear in the information given. This is not the responsibility of the listener!

In the above example, when I wanted Sandy to confirm that she did understand the information, I said, *"Sandy, I want to make sure I was clear in my instructions to you. Can you tell me the steps you'll be taking to complete this assignment?"*

Skill of Feedback:

Use feedback for both positive and negative situations. Use positive feedback to give recognition and compliments (covered in Chapter 4 - Motivation). We'll be concentrating here on using it under negative or difficult situations.

In feedback, you share your reactions to another person's behaviour, with that person. In other words, you discuss how you feel when others act or behave a certain way. People can't attempt to change their behaviour unless you let them know what their actions are doing to you. Letting things build up only escalates the difficulties between people. Resolve minor difficulties when they occur; don't accumulate them for future blowups.

Use feedback if you're upset or aggravated by something someone has done. You identify what they're doing that bothers you and give them the opportunity of doing something about it. We're being unfair to others when we don't communicate these issues to them.

If we don't practice effective feedback, the following often results:

- Every time the person does anything that bothers us, a small blip occurs on our "screen of annoyance." If we don't deal with the problem or situation, this leads to;
- Another, bigger blip appears on our "screen of annoyance." This does *not* have to be for the same reason as the original blip.
- Soon these blips accumulate, and we have a major blow-up with the person. The most trivial incident can trigger this response.

It would be much better if we handled each blip immediately to keep it from being recorded on our "screen of annoyance.

We can use feedback to:

- Let others know when you don't understand something they've said.
- Let others know when you like something they've said or done.
- Let others know when you disagree with them.

135

- Let others know when you think they've changed the subject or are going around in circles.
- Let others know when you're getting irritated.
- Let others know when you feel hurt or embarrassed.

With feedback you can keep in touch with your feelings and alleviate problems associated with more serious negative feelings. This is when you feel frustrated, angry, hurt, defensive, defeated, upset, afraid, depressed, dependent, weak or defenceless.

Most women are comfortable admitting these negative feelings, but society almost forbids men to admit to these weaknesses. Therefore, this limits their options for expressing their feelings. Many respond as if they're angry. This is an acceptable reaction among men. In reality, they may feel hurt, defenceless or afraid, but they still respond as if they're angry. This ambiguous behaviour confuses women and adds to the male/female communication gap. This gap will be reduced when everyone analyses what s/he is really feeling, before reacting.

Be selective when you use feedback. Ask yourself, *"Am I about to unload this beef properly? Is my reaction unfair or petty?"* Feedback must be recent and specific - not general, and the person must be able to do something about the situation.

To be effective, there must be a foundation of trust between the sender and receiver of the feedback. Otherwise, the feedback could be misinterpreted as a personal attack. The recipient may hear only critical things and defend him- or herself, rather than listen to what you have to say. Watch your timing - don't dump too many things on a person at once. Here are some guidelines for giving feedback:

a) Is the receiver ready? Give the feedback only when there are clear indications the receiver is ready to listen to it. If not ready, the receiver won't hear it or is likely to misinterpret your comments.

b) Based on facts - not emotions: Giving feedback acts like a "Candid camera." It's a report of the facts, rather than your ideas about why things happened or what the person meant by their actions.

c) Protect privacy: Critical feedback given in front of others will be damaging rather than helpful.

d) Must have happened recently: The closer you give feedback to the time the event took place, the better. If you give feedback immediately, the receiver is more likely to understand exactly what's meant. The feelings accompanying the event still exist so this, too, can help.

e) Timing must be right: Give feedback when there's a good chance the person will listen to it. It may not be helpful if the receiver feels there are already other matters that demand his/her attention.

f) They must be able to change Feedback should be about things that need changing should the receiver choose to do so. Freedom to decide: The receiver can consider whether s/he wishes to attempt a change on the basis of your feedback information.

g) Don't give too much at once: When learning how to give feedback, we may sometimes overdo it. It's as though we were telling the receiver, *"I just happen to have a list of reactions here. Let me read them off to you."* The receiver would naturally prefer time to consider each item and may balk at your high expectations.

h) Criticism should be helpful: Always consider your own motives for giving your opinions. Are you trying to be helpful to the receiver – or are you unloading some of your own feelings? Or are you using the occasion to try to get the receiver to do something that benefits only you? For example, if you're angry and wish to express it - say so - but include a description of the behaviour that caused your anger.

137

i) Encourage them to share feedback: Giving feedback can become "one-upsmanship." Because the giver has focused on the person's potential for improvement, the receiver goes away feeling as though s/he's "not as good." The receiver may feel you're giving him/her a lecture. The exchange will be better balanced if the giver includes some of his/her own feelings and concerns.

j) Be specific - not general: Give quotes and examples of exactly what you're referring to.

Here are some guidelines for receiving feedback:

a) State what you want feedback about: Help the giver provide useful reactions by asking for feedback about specific things.

b) Check what you've heard: Use paraphrasing to be sure you understand the giver's message. Because the topic is your own behaviour, you may think more about the meaning of the feedback than what it meant.

c) Share your reactions to the feedback: As your own feelings become involved, you may forget to share your reactions to the feedback you've received. Knowing what was and was not helpful assists the giver to improve his/her skills at giving useful feedback. If s/he is uncertain about your reactions, s/he may be less apt to risk sharing in the future.

Here is an example of how to use feedback:

A receptionist had a problem she didn't know how to handle. She would take messages for all the office staff. One particular client (Mr. Samuels) phoned in repeatedly asking to speak to Mr. Jacobs. She promptly passed on his messages. The fourth time he called, Mr. Samuels accused her of not passing on his messages to Mr. Jacobs. She wondered how she should deal with this situation, because it was likely to happen again. What would you suggest she tell Mr. Samuels the next time he phoned in?

Did you notice that she was trying to deal with the wrong problem? Her supervisor, Mr. Jacobs was the problem, not Mr. Samuels! I asked her if she had ever considered going in and talking to her supervisor to explain the problem she faced. *"Oh, I couldn't do that!"*

With that reply I asked, *"How is the situation going to change unless he knows what his behaviour is doing to you? You're not even giving him the opportunity of solving this dilemma."*

The three steps in the process of feedback are as follows:

Process of feedback

a) Describe the problem or situation to the person causing the difficulty.
b) Define what feelings or reactions (anger, sadness, anxiety, hurt or distress) the problem behaviour causes you.
c) Suggest a solution or ask the person to provide a solution.

In the receptionist's case, she might have felt like saying, *"You turkey, you never return your telephone messages!"* This would only get her supervisor's back up. Instead, she should try to gain his co-operation in solving the problem. She could say, *"I have a problem and I need your help in solving it. Mr. Samuels has phoned in five times, and he's really annoyed at me because you haven't returned his calls. This upsets me. What do you suggest I tell him the next time he calls?"*

When you do this, you're dumping the problem in the lap of the person who is causing it. It's done in such a nice way, that the person feels compelled to do something constructive about the problem. Using the process of feedback in the above situation:

a) Describe the problem or situation to the person causing the difficulty. *"He's not returning his phone messages."*
b) Define what feelings or reactions (anger, sadness, anxiety, hurt or distress) the problem behaviour causes you. *"This upsets me."*
c) Suggest a solution or ask the person to provide a solution. *She asks Mr. Jacobs to provide one.*

Here's another example:

Margo, a co-worker is always interrupting you with small talk, which affects your concentration. You're getting annoyed with her. Your first reaction might be to blast her with a statement such as, *"Margo will you shut up and let me get my work done!"* Use feedback instead and say, *"Margo, I'm working on an important project. I'm sure you're not aware of this, but every time you interrupt me, I lose my train of thought. Can we talk later at coffee break?"*

a) Describe the problem or situation to the person causing the difficulty. *"She's interrupting your work."*
b) Define what feelings or reactions (anger, sadness, anxiety, hurt or distress) the problem behaviour causes you. *"You lose your train of thought."*
c) Suggest a solution or ask the person to provide a solution. *"Can we talk later at coffee break?"*

If Margo interrupted you again two hours later, what should you tell her? (Remember, this might be a habit with Margo, and she may have done it without thinking).

Step 2 - repeat your original comments. *"As I mentioned earlier, I'm working on an important project. Every time you interrupt me, I lose my train of thought. Can we talk later at coffee break?"*

The next morning, guess what? She's at it again. What should you do now? Many would suggest that you ignore her comments. Instead say, *"Margo, twice yesterday I mentioned that I'm working on an important project and that your interruptions affected my concentration. Can you tell me why you're still doing this?"*

What you're doing is making Margo account for her aggressive actions. Yes, she's being aggressive, because she **knows** she's bothering you. Then explain that if it happens again, you'll have to speak to Jim, your supervisor. This is the step most people miss. It explains clearly the consequences Margo will face should she do it again. Margo promises she won't do it again.

Another day goes by and Margo's at it again! What should you do the fourth time? Don't just say you're going to do something - follow through and talk to your supervisor. (By the way, Jim, the supervisor was falling down on his supervisory duties and should have been aware of this problem.)

Rather than giving the impression that you're going to "tattletale" on your co-worker, ask for your supervisor's advice. Say*, "Jim, I have a problem and I need your help in solving it. On Tuesday, I spoke to Margo."* Explain everything you've done to stop her negative behaviour. Then you ask, *"What do you suggest I do next time she interrupts me?"*

Normally, he will talk to Margo himself, because Margo's wasting company money. As she reports to Jim, he's ultimately responsible for what she does and she's making him look bad.

You might ask yourself, *"Will Margo like me after I've spoken to my supervisor?"* Do you really care? She's going to cause you trouble whether you go to your supervisor or not.

Use the wording, *"I have a problem and I need your help in solving it,"* whenever someone is causing you grief. This is especially effective if used on the person who's causing the problem! You're not shaking your finger at them and bawling them out for their behaviour. This approach often gets the results you're after when other approaches fail. Use this feedback technique whenever a person's pen clicking, gum chewing, chair squeaking or loud voice affects your performance at work. Or this could be someone who is tardy in getting their information to you so you can complete your month-end report.

Non-Verbal Communication:

You can find books on this subject at the library under one of these three headings:

- Non-Verbal Communication;
- Body Language;
- Kinesics (Scientific name for the study of body language).

Space Bubbles:

We all have Space Bubbles of safety around us. To find yours:

Stand up extend our arms in front of you with overlapping hands together (makes an oval with your arms). Then with arms still extended, pivot around until you've made a full circle. You've just identified your space bubble. Normally, a person's space bubble is anywhere from 18 to 24 inches (forty to sixty centimetres) around his/her body. When someone ventures beyond this invisible barrier, we have physical reactions to it. The hair may rise on our arms or neck, and we have an irresistible urge to back away from a person invading our space.

There are several types of distances we normally keep between others and ourselves. These are:

- **Intimate distance.** Only people we trust are welcome within our space bubble. We welcome people who are near and dear to us into this space, but we often have to endure others as well. This can be at the theatre, on a bus, at a seminar or in a lift or elevator. You can probably think of hundreds of instances where we have to tolerate this closeness.

Watch yourself when you're in an elevator. You naturally pull in all your 'ends' and take up as little space as possible. Should you inadvertently touch the stranger next to you, you'll automatically say, *'Oops, sorry,'* and pull away. This would also happen if you touched someone in a bank line-up or at a checkout counter.

- **Personal distance** is the space you usually keep with others when you have enough room to be comfortable. This is anywhere between three and four feet (1 ½ metres) depending on your comfort zone and how well you know the person. In elevators, as soon as the crowd thins, people will automatically widen the space between themselves and others.

- **Social distance** is four to seven feet (1 1/2 to 2 metres). Strangers or acquaintances sitting on chairs or couches at a party will try to maintain this distance.

- **Far social distance.** This could happen at a large party or be the distance between a speaker and his or her audience.

Territory:

Many supervisors invade the space of their staff without knowing it. Hovering behind a person - peering over their shoulder at their work - is a definite invasion of their space. Don't do this: instead stand beside them to check their work.

Others help themselves to things on other's desks. Receptionists often fight a losing battle because others think it's their right to help themselves to whiteout, scissors and rulers off their desks. Some even have the boldness to open the desk drawer and help themselves to other items. Receptionists should order duplicates of these items and store them in a neutral zone, such as the top of a nearby filing cabinet.

Some use another's office when they're away (without permission). When the owner of the office returns, they know that someone has been "mucking about" with their belongings. Just having one thing out of place on their desk will tell them this. In their minds they own their desk, chair, filing cabinet etc., so don't invade that territory without permission.

Physical Clues:

A person may be verbally saying one thing - but their body language is saying another. Which should you pay attention to? You're right - to their non-verbal language. The only people who get away with this are con artists and compulsive liars because they've told the same lie so often that even they believe them, and their body language confirms their words.

Employees:

Watch your employees. Determine from their body language if they:

- Like what they're doing; or
- Feel good about themselves.
- Are they tired or full of energy? How do they walk, stand and sit?
- Are they depressed - happy?
- Are they lethargic - hyperactive?
- Are they nervous - calm?
- Are they agitated - quiet?
- Are they neatly groomed?
- Do they have good colour - could they be ill?
- Are they argumentative - or unduly quiet?

Take the time to really see your staff. Read everything you can on the topic of Body Language. I highly recommend one book, **The Silent Language** by Edward T. Hall that is helpful for those working with people from other cultures.

Now that you've improved your communication with others, it's time to tackle Problem solving and Decision-making.

CHAPTER SEVEN

PROBLEM SOLVING AND DECISION MAKING

We're constantly using the word "problem" in our daily lives. You would think that our everyday lives were nothing but problems. There are problems at work, with children, with money, car problems, health problems and even love problems. The list goes on and on.

A problem occurs if:

"A need, a wish, a desire, an objective or question appears, and we don't know the series of actions required to fill the void."

To solve a problem, the person must be clear about the following:

- The actual situation:
- The Gap: (The Problem):
- The Ideal Situation.

When they have a problem most people dive right in and try to solve their problem without thinking it through. Unfortunately, most just end up spinning their wheels, because they haven't taken the time to establish that they're tackling the right problem and have taken the necessary time to think things through.

Three criteria required for defining problems:

1. Specific Problem Definition:

Specific Problem: Must be detailed, quantitative and measurable.

General Problem: Is vague, difficult to measure.

145

Sample Situation - How to raise production levels:

This problem definition is too large and too general. Try breaking it down into smaller, more specific components.

Revised Example: How to motivate John smith so his work output improves by 20 percent before April 5, 20___.

2. Ownership of the Problem:

To establish ownership, you must ask yourself:

a) Is this problem mine or someone else's? (In the above case it *is* this person's problem because he's a supervisor, therefore he's ultimately responsible for the productivity of his staff).

b) Do I have the power and authority to put the solution into practice? Yes, he does - he's the employee's supervisor.

3. Personal Commitment to Solving the Problem:

The person needs to be willing to put forth the effort necessary to solve their problem.

Note: each problem statement must satisfy the above three criteria.

Next, define whether your problem is:

A short-term problem: 1 day, one month?
A long-term problem: More than one month?

A tangible problem: Something you can see, such as an object.
An intangible problem: Something you can't see, such as attitudes, feelings or behaviour.

Sample problem:

Here's a short-term problem. See how you think you would solve it:

146

You're leaving for work and find that your car will start, but it stalls and won't keep running properly.

The Specific Problem: (What is it?)

a)   To get my car started and running, or
b)   To get to work on time?

Ownership of the problem: (Do I own this problem? Yes!)

a) I need a method or way of keeping my car's engine running once it starts, or
b) I need to find a way to get to work on time (other than in my car).

Personal commitment to solving the problem: Am I willing to make the effort to solve this problem?

a)   I'm looking for ways to keep my car's engine running for a minimum of thirty minutes, or
b)   I'm looking for an alternative form of transportation to get me to work by 9:00 am, or
c)   I think I'll go back to bed (gives up - no commitment to solving the problem).

Dealing with your own problems:

To practice the process, identify a simple problem you've been wrestling with lately. When you've written it down, define whether it's specific enough (detailed, quantitative, precise, measurable) or was it too general (broad, vague, difficult to measure)

Was it a tangible problem (something you can see) or was it intangible (something you can't see)? As you've probably guessed, intangible problems are harder to solve, and solutions are much harder to evaluate.

Was your problem a short or long-term problem?

Here is a sample method to work through your problem. It's an aide to keep you from wasting valuable time. Unfortunately, most people waste time, energy and effort by trying to solve the wrong problem. This guide will help you determine the real problem:

Problem-solving and decision-making guide

(It's best to do this guide in pencil, because you'll probably change your mind on what really is the problem halfway through the process).

Step 1: The factual situation

Step 2: The ideal situation

Step 3: The problem (or cause of the gap)

Step 4: List the symptoms of the problem

- What's happening and why;
- Where it's happening and why:
- When it occurs and why:
- Who's involved and why:
- How it happens and why:

Step 5: List the Driving and Restraining forces

Driving Forces: (The benefits of solving the problem).

Restraining Forces: (Obstacles you must overcome to solve the problem).

Step 6: Identify how you will overcome the obstacles you've identified.

Step 7: List all the possible solutions to your problem - (brainstorm):

Step 8: Choose the best solution:

Step 9: Formulate an Action Plan:

- Steps or Actions:
- Date or time limit:

- People to Involve:
- Resources required:

Step 10: Implement your action plan.

Step 11: Evaluate the success of your action plan.

Here are several definitions that will help you understand the above method:

Driving Forces:
These are forces that are in favour of your problem being solved. They are the benefits that will result when you solve the problem.

Restraining Forces:
These are forces that are against your problem being solved. They are the things that stand in the way of getting your problem solved.

Brainstorming:

This is the process of generating ideas or creating solutions in either individual or group situations where the climate is free-wheeling and open. It is an ideal process all supervisors should use with their staff. Instead of spending three days mulling over a problem, get your staff involved. They'll likely come up with a solution in fifteen to twenty minutes (and probably a better one as well). Here's how you do this:

1. **Limit the topic to a single question**, e.g., how to deal with absenteeism.

2. **Encourage idea quantity**. At this point, don't consider quality of ideas. What you're seeking are as many ideas and suggestions as possible.

3. **Encourage wild thinking** - offer any idea (no matter how questionable). Encourage the group to build on one another's ideas, altering, expanding and modifying them.

Again, the purpose here is to get ideas - not to pass judgment on them.

4. **Discourage critical judgement and evaluation**. Don't allow anyone to say, *"That won't work because ..."* during a brainstorming session. You're looking for ways of getting ideas, not trying to suppress them. Someone's idea (that really won't work) might just be the thing that triggers someone else to think of one that *will* work.

   For example: In one of my sessions where I had explained this concept, the class received the following problem:

   My car is stuck in mud, what should I do?

   Everyone gave suggestions (both realistic and silly). An example of some of the funny suggestions were:

   - Bury my car;
   - Wait until the mud dries;
   - Sell my car;
   - Show a little leg (females);
   - Blow up my car.

   The last one gave the mental picture of a car flying up in the air and coming down in pieces. This prompted the suggestion:
   Jack up the car and push it off the jack. This bizarre suggestion triggered an excellent solution that I've used the idea to get my car out of mud one day.

5. **Avoid side discussion and issues**. During the actual brainstorming (which is of very short duration) don't allow side discussions. Ask all members of the group to concentrate their energies towards coming up with additional ideas.

6. **Don't allow outside observers.** Everyone in the room must participate. It may be wise to require everyone to offer at least two suggestions during the session.

7. **Have an idea or two in the back of your head** to provide a trigger to get the session moving. Once it begins, ideas come fast and furious.

8. One member of the group should **take notes,** recording the ideas as fast as they're offered. It's a good idea to have the suggestions listed on a flip chart or white board where everyone can see them. Previous ideas provide food for thought and lead to further ideas.

9. The brainstorming session itself **should not last** less than five minutes or more than fifteen. Shorter time doesn't allow enough good ideas to surface and after fifteen minutes, most of ideas become clearly impractical.

Tackling the wrong problem

I remember a time where a company had hired me to do a motivational seminar for their staff. They had a high turnover of staff and thought they required motivation to enjoy their jobs better. I conducted the one-day session which was well received by the participants. However, when I followed-up a while later, found that the turnover rate was still as high as before.

I asked the Human Resources person whether they had conducted exit interviews for the employees who had left. They had not done so. I asked whether I could conduct one on the employees who had left in the past two months and was given the go-ahead. In all cases, their reason for leaving was because of the terrible supervisor they all had reported to.

So, you see, the company did not investigate to see what was causing the low morale and overlooked the real reason for the turnover (a bad boss). They tackled the 'real' problem and the turnover stopped immediately.

Here's an example of how a person used the Problem Solving and Decision-making Guide:

Problem-solving and decision-making guide

Step 1: The factual situation

I'm having trouble getting along with my boss.

Step 2: The ideal situation

I'd like to get along with my boss.

Step 3: The problem (or cause of the gap)

He's inconsistent - changes his mind, so I don't know what he expects of me.

Step 4: List the symptoms of the problem.

What's happening and why:
I'm frustrated because I can't do a good job.

Where it's happening and why:
At the office - my boss is inconsistent and often changes his mind.

When it occurs and why:
When he gives me assignments, he doesn't seem sure of what he's to do; therefore, he has trouble delegating assignments to me.

Who's involved and why:
My boss and his boss (his boss starts the problem). Neither of them seem to be clear on what they want me to do.
How it happens and why:
Lack of clear directives from my boss.

Note: After answering these questions, it's clear that I've identified the "real" problem (not just the perceived one) so I have to go through the process again:

Step 1: The factual situation:

I don't know what my boss expects of me.

Step 2: The Ideal Situation:

To know what my boss expects of me.

Step 3: The problem (or cause of the gap):

Lack of clear directives from my boss

Step 4: (Complete this step again to confirm that your problem is the real problem.)

Step 5: List the driving and restraining forces.

Driving forces:

- *I'll know what I'm supposed to do.*
- *I can meet boss's needs.*
- *I can do a better job.*
- *I can risk-take more.*
- *I'll learn more.*

Restraining Forces:
- *I need communication skills.*
- *Could cause spin-off problems with boss if not done correctly.*
- *Could lose face with boss.*
- *Need the nerve to do it.*
- *Preparation time to do it.*

Step 6: Identify how you will overcome the obstacles you've identified.

- *Read some books on how to communicate better.*
- *Rehearse what I am going to say, so I feel comfortable doing so.*
- *Find a suitable time for both me and my boss to discuss this issue.*

Step 7: List all possible solutions - (Brainstorm):
- *Ask for written directions from my boss.*

- *Write boss's verbal directions down and confirm with him.*
- *Explain my frustrations to my boss and ask for his help.*
- *Find another job.*
- *Try to organise my boss.*
- *Ask for more information when project explained.*
- *Quit.*
- *Tell my boss what I think of his disorganisation.*

Step 8: Choose the best solution.
Explain my frustrations to my boss and ask for his help.

Step 9: Formulate an Action Plan

Steps or actions*: Make a list of my frustrations and possible solutions.*
Date or Time Limit: *Tonight.*
People to Involve: *Me.*
Resources Required: *Pen and paper, ideas, time.*

Steps or actions: *Ask for a meeting with my boss.*
Date or Time Limit: *Tomorrow.*
People to Involve: *Me, my boss.*
Resources Required: *Courage, my prepared list.*

Step 10: Implement Your Action Plan
Meeting held (date).

Step 11: Evaluate the success of your action plan.
*Much improved relations with my boss. He's as frustrated as I am at **his** lack of direction from **his** boss. Together we're formulating a plan initially to help him, then me.*

Note: There's now a new problem!

If you haven't worked out a problem on paper before, try this method with a simple problem. If you don't go through it, you won't be able to clarify in your mind that it really works.

154

Otherwise, it's possible that you'll spend far too much energy trying to solve the wrong problem.

It also gives you the opportunity of "walking through" the problem, without actually doing it. You'll be able to identify restraining forces that might get in the way of solving your problem. After identifying these restraining forces, you may decide that the time, energy and effort you'd need to spend, wouldn't be worth the results. You'll have saved yourself considerable grief by not actually trying to solve it (except on paper).

For other problems, you may find that you can get allies to help you. These are people who would be favourably affected if you solved the problem. Or you may decide that the problem isn't so earth-shattering after all. It helps to stop procrastination and keeps you moving forward towards finding solutions to problems.

Planning for problem-solving:

Let's say you've planned to take a business administration certificate program in the evenings at your local university. Taking two subjects per semester in the evening, you're looking at a number of years of hard work. This would be a long-term planning problem. Because it's a long-term project, you're discouraged about starting such a complex task or reluctant to make a commitment of this size.

If you break it down into small segments (one session at a time) you'll only have to deal with a portion of the overall project at one time. In the meantime, forget about the other subjects until it's time to take them. This way, you'll be able to give undivided attention to the one you're dealing with right now. You can then tackle portions of it, and it won't appear as overwhelming as you thought.

155

The Importance of Planning:

If proper planning is taken, the need for problem-solving may not occur in the first place.

Planning is thinking, writing and doing things in an orderly, systematic manner. Somehow, when you plan on paper, it takes on more importance and you're likely to follow-through with your plan. It helps you look ahead and make the best use of manpower, money, material and equipment.

Planning reduces guesswork from your job. Whether you build a plan quickly in your head or develop it slowly on paper, the method of planning is essentially the same.

Can you think of instances in your own work area where there was a lack of planning? What were some of the problems it caused? Here are examples of some that can happen due to lack of planning:

1. Reports are late;
2. Time is wasted;
3. Overtime necessary "to catch up;"
4. Results in bottlenecks to others;
5. Staff left with nothing to do while waiting for assignments;
6. Disorganised employees; and
7. Lost clients.

Planning Factors:

Planning what should be done each day, each week, each month can be tackled as follows:

Factor 1: What needs to be done?

Determine if the tasks planned for the day are, Routine, Periodic or Special. i.e.:

156

Routine: Those things that you do every day that might consist of keeping on top of regular work (uses 60 to 70 percent of your time).

Examples:

- Getting the day's work started.
- Checking work left over from yesterday.
- Giving information.
- Checking incoming mail and e-mail.

Periodic: Those duties or tasks that occur at regular intervals such as weekly, monthly, specific workday of the month etc. (Uses 20 to 25 percent of your time).

Examples:

- Weekly or monthly reports.
- Inventory checks.
- Staff meetings.
- Safety meetings.
- Updating job descriptions and
- Conducting Performance appraisals.

Special: Those things that you do to improve your work (can be above and beyond the call of duty). These could be ideas suggestions and proposed new ways of doing a task or special project.

Examples:

- Defining better ways of completing a task.
- Completing special projects.
- Setting up new policies and procedures.
- Revising or reducing reports or forms.

Write down all the routine, periodic and special duties that you do. Now do the same for your staff. If your company doesn't have job descriptions, you're well on your way to producing one!

Factor 2: How is task to be completed?

- What's your unit producing or servicing?
- What staff function is being offered?
- How does your manager measure your performance?

Factor 3: Who's to do it?

A job skills inventory sheet is often a good tool to answer this question. A job inventory can assist by:

- Showing turnover due to transfers, separations and retirements;
- Identifying vulnerable areas where there's a minimum coverage of responsibility;
- Establishing a training pattern for new workers; and
- Identifying the need for job rotation so you adequately cover all positions (especially because of illness).

Factor 4 - When should it be done?

- When is the best time to do it?
- Should you combine it with other tasks?
- Should you have it done before or after some other tasks?

Factor 5 - Where's it to be done?

- Where's the task being done?
- Where else could it be done?
- Where's the best place to do it?

Factor 6 - What results are achieved?

- Cross-training eliminates vacancies due to illness;
- Bottlenecks are eliminated;

158

- Fewer surprises;
- Fewer crisis; and
- Better utilisation of staff, materials and money.

Job Skills Inventory Chart:

Factor 3 mentioned a Jobs Skills Inventory Chart. Here's a sample job skills inventory chart for a Mail Room Unit.

Worker: Bill Adams
Responsibilities: Addressograph, Machine maintenance

Worker: Pat Elum
Responsibilities: Mail sorting, Word Processing

Worker: Stan Ward
Responsibilities: Postage Machine

Worker: Lyle Harris
Responsibilities: Mail delivery

Worker: Mary Mooney
Responsibilities: Mail sorting, Postal Zones

Worker: Helen Pepper
Responsibilities: Word processing

Worker: Frank Ricker
Responsibilities: Mail sorting, Machine maintenance

Worker: Chuck Sweeney
Responsibilities: Mail Sorting, Postage Machine, Postal Zones, Machine Maintenance

Worker: Clara Anders
Responsibilities: Word Processing

As you examine this job skills inventory chart, what are some strengths and weaknesses of this group should concern the supervisor?

Strengths:

- Lots of word processors (too many?)

- 3 machine maintenance people.
- Relief help for mail sorting, postage machine and postal zoning.

Weaknesses:

- Too many responsibilities for Chuck?
- No relief for mail delivery and addressograph operator.
- Boredom for Stan, Helen, Clara and Lyle.

Complete a Job Skills Inventory Chart for your area. What discrepancies does it point out? Should you be contemplating job rotation or cross-training? What if one of your staff was sick, could you place another experienced worker in his/her place? Many workers object to this, but what they're likely objecting to is their fear of change. To overcome this fear of change:

The Change Process:

People go through four basic stages when they have changes made in anything they do. Supervisors and trainers must be aware of this, because they will "slip back" to doing it the old way if not stopped.

1. **Unfreezing**: Happens when you "unfreeze" their regular way of doing things that allows the acceptance of new ideas. This involves breaking down of old ways of doing things and can involve customs and traditions.
2. **Changing**: This provides a new pattern of behaviour, identifies a new way of doing something. Before approaching anyone with a change, identify the driving forces and find ways to overcome the restraining forces. Describing the advantages of the new system is essential for success.
3. **Refreezing**: The new idea replaces the old one and the new way is "frozen", so employees don't revert to the old

160

way. Die-hards will resist and try to do it the "old way" so you must be wary of these people.

4. **Commitment**: People are ready to make plans that utilise the new way, to set and implement long-range plans.

When implementing a change, you feel may meet with resistance (and even those you don't) do advance planning. Make a list of:

1. Driving forces in favour of the plan succeeding and benefits that will result (brainstorm).
2. Restraining forces against the plan succeeding and things standing in the way (brainstorm).
3. Find solutions to restraining forces.
4. Put solution on paper for easy reference.
5. Introduce the change.
6. Evaluate the effectiveness of your planning and the change itself.

New systems, methods and designs won't work unless you get people to accept new ideas, so you may have to sell your ideas. This is where planning comes in.

For Example: You've found a faster way to process client's orders. Before explaining the new system to others, prepare by:

- Writing down the existing way. (Its advantages and disadvantages).
- Writing down the new way (Its advantages and disadvantages).

Anticipate that George will object by saying *"But we've always done it this way. Twenty people will have to learn a new way of doing it."*

Your answer could be (giving concrete facts) *"Here's how much time we'll save by doing it the new way. I've determined that we'll save 5 minutes per order. As there are about 1,000 orders processed per month that's a saving of 5,000 minutes or*

250 minutes per employee per month. This means that every employee will have an extra 4 hours and 10 minutes to work on other tasks per month. This amounts to a saving of $_____."

George is unlikely to have his facts ready. Remember, if the new procedure doesn't work - you won't look good - so do considerable planning before you try to activate changes.

Meeting objections head-on:

The following checklist will help you cope with objections more effectively.

1. Pinpoint the objection - spell it out in clear and concise language.
2. Don't take the voiced objections of others for granted. People sometimes voice one complaint to mask another they'd prefer to conceal.
3. Work out a practical way of erasing the objection if possible.
4. If you're unable to remove it, try to find a way to counteract it.
5. Anticipate and prepare for as many possible objections as you can. Develop a plan for handling each. (Rehearse).
6. Rally enough benefits to win the person's support and co-operation despite the objection.
7. Try to find a way to get around the objection or to minimise its adverse affect.
8. Collect as much irrefutable evidence as you can, to convince the person you're trying to sell that his/her objection is unreasonable (if such is the case).
9. Find a way to ease the person's mind, by making it less risky to go along with you despite their objection.
10. Spoon-feed your idea or proposal on a gradual basis.
11. Don't try to get immediate acceptance or compliance. The objection may be nothing more than a delaying tactic, the person's natural resistance to change.

12. Consider bringing up significant objections yourself instead of waiting for the other person to do it.

Making changes happen

Here's a guide that you can use when making changes (it's similar to the problem-solving guide) to help you deal with change. Write down:

Step 1: The existing way

We have 40 parking stalls available for staff parking.

Step 2: The proposed new way

We must reduce this number to 30 parking stalls.

Step 3: Identify how it is done now.

What's happening?
We have 40 parking stalls available for staff parking.
Where is it happening?
In the staff parking area.
When it occurs?
Daily parking provided for 3 shifts (120 staff)
Who's involved?
Senior staff
How does it happen?
Seniority list determines those who can have stalls.

Step 4: Identify the proposed new way:

What's happening?
We have only 30 parking stalls available for staff parking (reduction of 10 stalls).
Where is it happening?
In the staff parking area.
When it occurs?
Daily parking provided for 3 shifts (90 staff). (30 staff will have to find parking elsewhere).
Who's involved?

163

Senior staff
How does it happen?
Seniority list determines those who can have stalls.

Step 5: List the Driving Forces (Benefits when the change is made)

- No confusion as to who will or will not have a parking stall.
- We'll be able to use the extra space for visitors (clients).
- Less hostility from clients and customers because visitor parking will now be available.

Step 6: List the Restraining Forces (Obstacles to making the change)

a) 30 staff who have parking stalls will have to find parking elsewhere.
b) Problems with union.
c) Sour grapes and possible sabotage on the part of employees.
d) Resentment towards those who still have parking stalls.
e) Guilt feelings on the part of those who still have parking stalls.

Step 7: List all the possible solutions to solve the restraining forces (Brainstorm)

a) Make a list of alternative parking in the area.
b) Have a meeting with the union representatives - ask for their co-operation during implementation of the change.
c) Call a meeting with affected employees to explain the reasons for the change (better customer relations - increased sales and profits). Explain that you will pay for their parking at an alternative nearby site.

d) Provide an extra perk to those losing parking stalls - possibly give each person who has to go to an alternative site a fire extinguisher or first-aid kit for their vehicle.
e) There shouldn't be any guilt feelings if the above is put into place.

Step 8: Formulate an Action Plan:

Step or Action: *Determine which employees will have to give up parking stalls*
Date or Time Limit: *Today*
People to Involve: *Me*
Resources Required: *Seniority list*

Step or Action: *Find and choose alternative parking*
Date or Time Limit: *Tomorrow*
People to Involve: *Personal Assistant*
Resources Required: *Time*

Step or Action: *Meet with union representatives*
Date or Time Limit: *Tomorrow*
People to Involve: *Union Reps – me*
Resources Required: *Time, preparation*

Step or Action: *Obtain samples of fire extinguishers and first aid kits*
Date or Time Limit: *Friday, the 6th*
People to Involve: *Personal*
Resources Required: *Time, cost of samples*

Step or Action: *Call meeting with affected employees*
Date or Time Limit: *Monday the 9th*
People to Involve: *Employees, me*
Resources Required: *Preparation, List of options*

Step 9: Implement your action plan
Meeting with employees held (date)

Step 10: Evaluate the success of your action plan

Employees were upset initially, but when they learned that we would pay for nearby parking for them and provide either a fire extinguisher or first aid kit for their vehicles they agreed to accept the change.

Conflict Resolution:

Whenever conflict occurs, it's helpful to consider the four basic approaches to resolving conflicts:

Competition Approach: These are:
"Win-Lose" situations - One person or group wins, the other loses.
"Might makes right" - This could be the status of a person in a company.
"Winner takes all" - Another win-lose situation.
"Survival of the Fittest" - One-upsmanship.

Accommodation Approach: These are:

"Yield-lose" situations - Passive behaviour. Person doesn't actively participate.
"Kill your enemies with kindness." - This too is passive – a form of passive resistance.

Compromising Approach: These are:
"Sharing, negotiating, bargaining."
"Win some - lose some."
"Splitting the difference."
"You rub my back - I'll rub yours."
"Democracy."

Collaboration Approach: These are:
"Let's work together" – teamwork.
"Two heads are better than one."

The last one - Collaboration Approach is the best conflict resolution approach. There are no competitive feelings in this approach, rather a feeling of co-operation between members of the team - camaraderie. All members are open to negotiate. This attitude uses all the talents of the group without losing the individualities of the members. There are no negatives - only positives. It's a win-win approach.

Creative problem-solving:

We're all born full of creativity. Criticism of our behaviour slowly but surely stops this creativity and affects our self-image. Then at school, children are encouraged to become clones - to fit in - to lose their individuality, which stifles creativity even more. Those that do not conform receive labels like: "radical, wave-makers, extremist, militant, fanatical, rebellious, revolutionary or different."

We use our right brain for our creative ideas. This includes visual memory (remembers the face, but not the name) artistic talent and creativity. Our left side does the analytical thinking that relates to language and logic.

We're split in half - one half keeps us safe (the safekeeping self) and the other is the part that yearns for everything (our experimental self). These segments are often at war with each other.

Brainstorming was a tool devised to assist in creative problem solving. Initially, most of those who used the technique were men. This technique proved moderately successful until a manager couldn't make it to a meeting, so sent his secretary to take notes for him. Since everyone had to participate, she contributed as well. The managers couldn't believe the outcome - she came up with two of the four workable suggestions. They couldn't understand why her answers were better than those of professionals who understood all aspects of the problem.

At the next meeting, they tried an experiment. All the managers brought their secretaries to the meeting. Most of the ideas again came from the women! The women didn't censor their own ideas as critically as the men. Before speaking, most men generally examined their ideas to see if they are "good enough" before submitting them to the group. Some did this out of a fear of looking silly and some because they couldn't turn off the self-censoring mechanism that told them, *"That won't work."*

In this case, the women were instructed to let ideas flow unrestricted - so they did. They suggested any idea they could think of. It didn't matter whether it was a good idea, because they knew their suggestions would be evaluated after the brainstorming session.

If the men had practiced listening to their "gut reactions" the way the women listened to their "intuitions" they wouldn't have had this problem. Many businesses now make sure half the participants in creative problem-solving sessions are women.

Let your "little kid" out and allow your creative juices to flow. You'll be surprised how effective it is - not only thinking up advertising campaigns or marketing a product - but in finding creative solutions to difficult problems. It will allow you to take something that is average and make it superior.

We'll now go on to solving another problem - that of adequately training your staff so they can do a good job for you.

CHAPTER EIGHT

TRAINING AND DEVELOPMENT

Qualities of a good trainer:

Trainers need many qualities to be successful. Some are used by those researching and preparing seminars. For instance:

1. Good research ability;
2. Attention to detail;
3. Ability to determine training needs;
4. Ability to prepare a seminar to meet those training needs;
5. Ability to sift through research material and take out only what is applicable;
6. Good knowledge of training methods;
7. Good sense of timing - able to time segments to keep learners interest;
8. Ability to prepare interesting sessions with variety and different methods of presenting material; and
9. Well organised.

Those who actually present seminars require the following qualities:

1. Interested in people;
2. Like dealing with people;
3. Knowledge of the subject being taught;
4. Good verbal and presentation skills;
5. Self-assured;
6. Well organised;
7. Empathetic to others;
8. Good listener;
9. Ability to "bring out" quiet participants;
10. Ability to create an atmosphere of learning;
11. Does not threaten participants;
12. "In tune" with the mood of the group;

169

13. Ability to explain information and skill knowledge in a clear, concise manner that is clearly understood by the participants;
14. Ability to read others' body language;
15. Ability to "ad lib;"
16. Sense of humour;
17. Adaptable;
18. Perceptive;
19. Patient;
20. Radiates confidence;
21. Punctual, prepared and professional;
22. Good physical appearance; and
23. High energy level.

#21 is crucial to the success of a presenter. It's unforgivable for a trainer to be late for a session. If they're not properly prepared - all they do is waste everyone's time. If they don't conduct themselves professionally, they won't gain the respect of the audience, nullifying the content of the training session. Many adult learners would simply leave the session.

Teaching Adults:

As people grow older, it becomes more and more difficult to change established behaviour. Society has often encouraged people to be closed-minded towards new ideas. The creativity curve in most children levels off between six and eight years of age. This is when society dumps more negative criticism on children than positive. Therefore, when they become adults, they're often much more comfortable with negative criticism than with praise. They're used to feeling bad, rather than good about themselves.

If you've been trained as a teacher of children, you'll likely "bomb" at teaching adults, because an entirely different approach is necessary. Adults feel that this type of instructor "talks down to them." Teachers would be more in tune and perceptive if they treated child learners in this manner as well.

170

Children respond better if they're treated as if they were "little adults."

As trainers, your major responsibility may be to overcome the negative feelings your participants obtained in school as a child. This is accomplished by providing an atmosphere conducive to learning with low-risk factors for the individuals.

Many people resist taking responsibility for their actions and their own futures. The book "The Cinderella Complex" by Collette Dowling describes this phenomenon in women. It explains how most women, live their lives under the assumption that someone else will look after them. Therefore, they have difficulty making any decision without getting the advice of at least one other person. They, in effect, resist taking responsibility for their actions and therefore their futures as well.

As a trainer, you'll need to overcome this obstacle. Men, too, may drift into this. They let the "organisation" or "Big Brother" make all their work decisions for them - to determine their career paths. They float through life, making few direct decisions for themselves.

Our present social system heavily encourages dependence, conformity, submission and role-playing as the norm. Others follow their urges and grow, take risks, change and take charge of their lives and destiny. Sometimes, though, this growth and change can be painful.

For instance, an employee attends a workshop on "Interpersonal Skills" - returns to work but run into difficulties. S/he's anxious to use his/her new skills but finds his/her co-workers and supervisor sceptical of his/her actions. Often s/he's forced to revert back to his/her old pattern (even if it was a bad one) so s/he doesn't "make waves." Follow-up sessions will enable trainers to see whether participants were able to use the skills effectively in their work environment.

As instructors, you'll need to be in tune with the objectives of the group - be able to motivate them to learn the necessary information and new skills. It takes a particular kind of person to do this.

Giving training as a "reward or a perk" for good performance or because George hasn't had any training this year; are poor reasons for sending anyone to training sessions. Training should be for specific reasons only.

Try to make sure attendees are there because they desire and need the training being offered. It's a good idea to determine the driving and restraining forces that might be in place for the trainees. One restraining force to learning might be a heavy workload that's piling up while they attend the training. Try to have someone take over their duties while they're away so they can concentrate on the training.

Determine at the beginning of the session why each of them feels the training session they're at will benefit them (learner's objectives). You might find out as I did that half the participants of an in-house training program were there under duress. Some may not have known they were to attend the seminar until the day before the session started.

If you have to face this kind of situation, say, *"I know some of you are here under duress and didn't ask for this training. I'd like you to decide whether you're going to put in time here at this session or are you going to "fool them and learn something?"* I tried this and was surprised by the positive results. I had given the choice back to the participants. They now could choose what their attention level would be during the seminar. Most decided to *"fool them and learn something."*

Characteristics of adult learners:

In general, there are certain characteristics that distinguish adult learners from child learners.

1. Most adults are highly motivated to learn as long as it applies to their needs.
2. Adults like to take part in determining their own training needs.
3. Adults like sequential learning, with graduated stages of learning - lots of feedback and re-enforcement from their trainer.
4. Adults enjoy novelty in learning - but can be "turned off" or frightened by some ideas if they're too far out.
5. Adults have difficulty being re-trained; have set ideas on how to do things. Trainers need to show them why the new idea or method is superior to the old one.
6. An authoritarian set-up for learning is not acceptable and often increases the risk factor.
7. Learning will be retained if it's used as soon as possible.
8. Adults have set patterns of behaviour - this pattern has to be "unset" in order for learning to take place.
9. Adults usually require a longer time to "lock-in" and do tasks a different way.
10. Adults are less tolerant of "busy work" which doesn't have immediate or direct application to their own objectives.
11. The older adult may have restricted powers of adjustment to external forces and distractions. They require more constant and ideal environmental conditions in order to learn or work efficiently.
12. Because adult learners are typically evening or "after work" students, they're more likely to be physically and mentally tired. This makes them less alert when coming to class. This, however, is offset by their increased desire to learn.
13. Adults have more experience in living, which gives them the advantage of being more readily able to relate new facts to experience.
14. Training is mainly a voluntary decision for them, and their attendance often represents a considerable sacrifice.

Having made this important and commendable decision, they expect (and deserve) the trainer's respect and to be treated as adult learners.

Differences in adult and child learners:

1. Adults are more realistic. They've lived longer and have a different perspective of life. They no longer see life through rose-coloured glasses, but as a set of realities.
2. Adults have had more experience. They have insights and see relationships not discerned by children. They've accumulated wisdom that gives them a sense of what's likely to work and what's not.
3. Adults have needs that are more concrete and immediate than those of children. They're impatient with long discourses on theory and like to see theory applied with practical solutions.
4. Adults are not a captive audience. They attend voluntarily and if their interest is lacking, they're inclined to stop attending.
5. Adults expect to be treated as mature persons and resent having instructors talk down to them.
6. Adults enjoy having their talents and abilities recognised and to be given the opportunity to enhance them during a teaching situation.
7. Adult groups are likely to be more diversified than youth groups. Differences increase with age and mobility. Therefore, adult learners come from a wider variety of backgrounds.
8. Adults, through their fifties and beyond, can learn as well as youth. They may not perform some assignments as rapidly as children because of a slowing up of physical functions.
9. Adults attend classes often with a mixed set of motives - educational, social, recreational and sometimes out of a sense of duty.

10. Adults may be tired when attending classes. They appreciate teaching devices that add interest and liveliness such as variety of methods, audio-visual aids, change of pace or sense of humour.

Learning process:

Learning involves personal change, which each trainee responds to differently. Motivation is the most important factor of learning. People learn what they want to learn, when they want to learn and under what conditions. Keeping up with or ahead of their peer group may be a motivator. It could simply be the need to learn, to keep advancing or to earn more money.

If the conditions of learning are not satisfactory the training might be a waste of time. These conditions could be:

- Room too hot or too cold;
- Chairs uncomfortable;
- Too much distracting noise;
- Lights too bright (usually fluorescent);
- Not enough variety in learning;
- They're there under duress or pressed for time;
- They have a feeling of failure due to the atmosphere or the style of instruction.

The ability to learn has its limitations because of the person's motor skills or level of intellect. A trainee learns best by participating in the learning process. The learner must be able to predict where they will use the learning. Describe similarities in different ways until they recognise and understand the connection of the learning material to their personal situation.

How to "lock-in" training:

Unless verbal data is repeated many times, it will be poorly retained. A combination of verbal and written material is far superior for retention of information by the trainee. Keep in mind that trainees retain:

- 10% of what they read (handouts, manuals).
- 20% of what they hear (have explained to them).
- 30% of what they see done (demonstrations).
- 40% of what they read and hear.
- 50% of what they read, hear and see demonstrated.
- 70% of what they read, hear, see demonstrated and they explain what they will do.
- 90% of what they read, hear, see demonstrated, they explain what they will do and then demonstrate themselves.

Here's how you utilise the above information:

1. Trainer gives handout, which shows the steps participants will take to complete the task (10% retention).
2. Trainer explains the information on the handouts (20% retention).
3. When you combine #1 and #2 the retention is 40%
4. Trainer demonstrates to the trainee how to complete the task (30% retention).
5. When you use all three of the above (50% retention).
6. In addition to 5, ask the trainee to use paraphrasing to explain verbally what they're going to do (70% retention).
7. In addition to 5 and 6, trainee demonstrates for the trainer how s/he will complete the task.

This method uses the trainee's sight, hearing and touch senses. It encourages learners to be better listeners. This is because they know that there'll be a test during the training. Give learner written back-up information for future reference and have them use the training as soon as possible.

Recall is another training fundamental. Some may forget the overall training but can recall something they've learned which stimulates more memory of the issues taught in the course. An atmosphere of approval and acceptance where participants can offer ideas and confirm their thought-patterns relating to the issues is essential for true learning.

Refresher training courses re-enforce the original information given but are usually presented in a more capsulated form. One also tends to repeat behaviour that seems to bring rewards and not repeat behaviour that seems to be without reward or to bring punishment.

For example, a test is given, and errors are corrected. Using positive feedback the trainer would say, *"You had the majority of it right. This is the only area where you went astray."* Concentrate on what they did right, not what they did wrong!

Determining training needs:

Training needs must be established before writing or implementing any training program. This is normally the job of the researcher or the person preparing the training package or manual. You can determine training needs by or from:

1. Performance appraisals that have a section relating to training needs.
2. Exit interviews - may identify that the employee left because the company didn't meet his/her training needs.
3. Supervisors identify performance problems.
4. Clients - usually in the form of complaints.
5. Organisational requirements - new equipment, policies, procedures or new ways of doing things company-wide.
6. Union requirements.
7. Technological advances - to upgrade employee's knowledge - usually an on-going occurrence in most companies.
8. Recruiters - the gap between qualification of candidates and the requirements of the position.
9. Employees themselves ask for training.

10. Production/work output - problems or new methods determined.
11. Morale problems.
12. Company questionnaires.
13. Accident statistics.

You may have identified the following that have training needs:

- Individuals for personal upgrading.
- Group needs (learning how to use a new computer); or
- Organisation-wide training (such as implementation of a new performance appraisal system).

Testing abilities of employees:

To determine individual needs for training, a company may administer the following more objective tests:

a) **General intellectual abilities**: These are not typical I.Q. tests but are more job-related and determine verbal comprehension and reasoning abilities.

b) **Aptitude tests**: Determine a person's capacity to obtain new levels of knowledge, skills and attitudes from training.

c) **Achievement tests**: Measures what an employee knows, understands or can do in relation to specific areas of knowledge or skill.

d) **Motor skill tests:** Involve physical agility, manual dexterity and sense of hearing, vision and touch. These are used where motor abilities are essential for successful completion of duties of a position.

e) **Interests and motivation tests**: Are difficult tests to assess because people tend to give answers, they think are expected of them. To obtain correct assessment, questions must be skilfully worded. The person evaluating these tests requires considerable training themselves.

f) **Interpersonal and leadership skills**: Assessed from work history and references from present and former supervisors.

g) **Personal history data:** Begins with the application form or resume and information from an employee's personnel file. This information includes previous education, experience, credentials, membership and occasionally reference checks.

h) **Current performance and potential**: Assessed by performance appraisals and employee's capability for learning.

Dimensions tested:

These are more subjective and only used in conjunction with objective information gathered. They are valuable for determining training needs in areas that are not as tangible to evaluate as objective ones:

1. **Speaking ability**: Ability to effectively express oneself in both individual and group situations.
2. **Listening ability**: Ability to pick out important information in oral communication.
3. **Writing ability**: Ability to express ideas in a clear, concise, grammatically correct manner.
4. **Reading ability**: Ability to obtain facts and comprehend meaning in written communication.
5. **Ability to analyse**: Ability to identify and interpret the key elements of a situation, concept or problem.
6. **Judgement**: Ability to evaluate situations and/or information and reach logical conclusions.
7. **Decisiveness**: Readiness to make decisions on the basis of sound judgment.
8. **Plan and organise**: Ability to effectively plan and organise their own work and direct or assist others in planning and organising their work.

9. **Delegate:** Ability to delegate tasks in a manner conducive to effectiveness and subordinate development.
10. **Control**: Ability to effectively use administrative controls for evaluation, auditing and monitoring functions.
11. **Leadership**: Ability to guide a group or individual to where they can effectively accomplish a task.
12. **Flexibility**: Ability to modify their approach and/or behaviour as required.
13. **Empathy**: Awareness, understanding and consideration of the needs and feelings of others.
14. **Initiative**: Ability to motivate themselves to take positive action and have a "sense of urgency."
15. **Tolerance to stress**: Ability to maintain expected performance levels under stress.
16. **Co-operative philosophy**: Ability to perceive and show positive reaction to current needs and future expectations of the company.
17. **Creativeness**: Ability to generate imaginative solutions to problem situations.

Manpower planning:

When determining training needs it's important to evaluate the present situation. Companies use manpower planning to compare the demands of the corporation vs. the supply of manpower available. This defines immediate needs and establishes long-range requirements.

Demand: Refers to the perceived demands of an organisation determined by budgetary requests, predicted expansions and changes in technology (usually determined in five-year forecasts).

Supply: The existing supply of manpower less turnover, retirement, attrition, etc. Often companies have senior people who are ready to retire. They suddenly realise there's no one to replace them or they realise there'll be a gap if they promote someone to a higher level. Manpower planning keeps this from happening and uses and expands the skills of existing employees.

Training needs of supervisors:

The supervisor who finds that s/he is constantly describing his/her staff as "second rate" is in essence, describing his/her own performance. This supervisor's not providing the proper training guidelines and motivation for co-operation of his/her employees. Many of these supervisors haven't had the basic training required to do their own jobs properly. Or it's possible their manager didn't have the basic training required to get the job done.

Supervisors have the responsibility of not only delegating work, checking work, etc., but to:

- Identify training needs;
- Provide on-the-job training;
- Help develop training programs; and
- Take part in training to meet the needs of any new policy or technology that affects his/her staff.

It's not enough to provide the above to employees. The employees, themselves must:

- Be willing to perform: Resistance can be cultural, personal, an unwillingness to take risks; work environment may not be conducive (kind of supervision etc.) types of employees or general work attitudes. The supervisor's or manager's attitude controls seventy-five percent of this area.
- Have the ability to perform: Correct this by offering proper training. Make sure the training is offered to both men and women.
- Have the Opportunity: Could be self generated (employee asks for the opportunity) or their supervisor offers it for

developmental purposes or through necessity for the employee to stay on the job.

Learning a new skill:

Teaching someone a new skill takes talent and perseverance. Use of paraphrasing helps implant information. As learners, we all pass through four definite stages when learning something new. These stages are:

Unconscious Incompetence - They aren't even aware that they lack the skill. For example - they may not even have known that the skill of Paraphrasing existed.

Conscious Incompetence - They're aware that they lack the skill. For example, before they learned how to drive a car, they knew they couldn't drive a car.

Conscious Competence - They know the techniques of the skill but had to stop and think before they reacted. *"Do I push the clutch in first or do I turn on the key first?"*

Unconscious Competence - The skill is now well established and automatic. They probably don't even think about what they're doing when they drive - they're on "automatic pilot."

It takes six weeks to "lock into" how to do something new and up to three months to "lock-into" doing something differently than the way they used to.

Retention of information:

Those who're responsible for training have probably thrown their hands in the air at times. Their information seems to go in one ear and out the other with some learners. Many people require constant repetition of instructions. This type of person is probably a poor listener.

Information has a better chance of being "locked in" when trainers use a variety of training methods. This could be with visual aides such as movies, PowerPoint presentations or flip charts. To further "lock in" the training, see that they use the training as soon as possible.

Training of others:

If you've had the responsibility of training others, you've probably had to explain how to do something more than once. Paraphrasing is a very effective tool to use when training others, especially if they're lazy listeners. To help them retain their training, do the following:

1. Give them short, sequential instructions.
2. State, *"To make sure that I was clear in my instructions to you, could you please explain what you're going to do?"*
3. If they give you a blank look and are unable to relate the steps.
4. Repeat the short, sequential instructions.
5. Again, ask them to relate the steps they will take to complete the task.

You'll find that their listening skills will improve immeasurably. They'll know that when you train them to do anything new, there'll be a *test* to see if they've listened properly. You'll find that instruction-giving will be much easier for you in the future.

Do; however, remember that the onus is on you to make your instructions clear. Using such questions as:

"Do you understand?" (This doesn't confirm that they did understand what you asked them to do).
"Explain what I want you to do." (This will just get their backs up).
"Did you catch that?" (This is a put-down, because you're insinuating that they aren't bright enough to pick up the information).

If they misunderstand you, it's much better to make the problem yours. You can accomplish this by statements such as:

"So, I'm sure I was clear in my instructions to you ..."
"Let's see if I've been clear in my instructions to you."

Then ask if they have any questions to clarify the training.

Training vs. development:

Training Need: Exists any time employees require updating of existing skills or need to learn new ones.

Developmental Need: Deals with the full utilisation of the skills of every employee. It uses the abilities learned during training or uses the innate skills of each employee. It's excellent for motivating employees to do their very best and can assist them to reach the "self actualisation" level in motivation.

Development:

When you think of the development of people, what do you usually think of? Formal training, probably. If employees require development, we think of sending them off somewhere else to attend classes, courses, conferences, workshops and seminars. 87 percent of a person's development takes place on the job and the person's boss is the most important teacher in his/her work life.

Compare development to an elastic band. It expands the knowledge learned in training. Unless a person expands his/her horizons, s/he won't be able to stretch when necessary. Developmental opportunities come up during a normal day, but we often don't think of them as developmental. Let's see if you can identify development vs. training. Assume that your boss said the following things to you. Which statements do you see as Developmental (D) and which as Training (T):

1.   What would you recommend?
2.   I'm going to show you how our new computer system works. You'll be using it from now on.

3. Tell me only what you feel I should know about your operations and why you feel I should be aware of these things.
4. I'm not going to make your decisions for you, but I'll certainly discuss your problem with you whenever you wish.
5. I'd like you to attend the meeting on safety that all the employees are attending.
6. Please attend this planning meeting in my place. You know our goals and have full authority to commit us to whatever course of action you feel is appropriate.
7. You didn't make the decision to cancel the project soon enough. Let's review it together, to see what we should have done to reduce our losses.
8. Here's a special project for you that will give you experience in a new area. When you finish a plan for accomplishing it, bring it in and show me what you suggest doing.
9. The head of our treasury group mentioned the fine co-operation he has been getting from you. Keep up the good work.
10. Here's a book on management that I just read. When you've had a chance to read it, let's get together and discuss it. We may find ways of improving our operations.

Only numbers 2 and 5 involved training - the rest are developmental. How did you do?

Career development:

On-the-job career development occurs under these conditions:

- Job rotation;
- Special tasks;
- Acting capacity for more senior position;
- Asked for advice;
- Team effort;
- Allowed to make decisions;

- Problem solving;
- New duties; or
- Assist supervisor in tasks.

Training procedure:

Follow this procedure to set up a training plan to meet training needs:

1. **List problems.** Most training requirements surface when problems occur. Examine these problems to see if they are the real problems.

2. **Determine training needs** to delete problems.
   Here are some Sample Training Needs:
   a) Problem solving capability of several employees requires improvement.
   a. Employees must learn how to handle change or new situations.
   b. Communication skills require improvement.
   c. Work ethic and attitude towards work needs to change.
   d. Establish orientation program to help employees understand the organisation better.
   e. Employees must learn how to use our new computer.
   f. Supervisors need to learn how to delegate and motivate their subordinates better.
   g. Time management problems due to overdue reports and work overloads.
   h. Third shift being put into place - train full crew in the use of the equipment.

3. **Set training objectives** to meet training need.
   These objectives must be realistic and within the scope of learning of the group or person being trained. The objectives must be specific (tangible - easy to measure) rather than general (intangible - difficult to measure). For instance:

General Objective: Improve interpersonal skills of employee.

Specific Objective: List 8 steps in the communication process.

Objectives require several pieces of information to be valid (quality, quantity, and time). When setting objectives, ask yourself - what is it I want the learner to be able to do after training? After setting the objectives, determine the conditions under which you expect the result to occur: Such as:

    a. Given a list of ...

    b. Without the aid of notes ...

    c. On the job ... Or

    d. Whatever help you provide or deny the participant such as: after five hours of dual flight time, the student will be able to land the airplane safely without help from the instructor.

4. **Conditions:** After 5 hours of dual flight time, following all safety and flight rules and without help from the instructor, participant will be able to ...

5. **Minimal level of achievement**: Will be able to land the airplane safety without help from the instructor.

6. **Write training program.** Consider the following when writing a training program:

    a. Participants: Size of group, familiarity with subject and their sex (females participate in class participation portions more than men) age, ethnic makeup, belief systems, voluntary/mandatory attendance.

    b. Fun: Be creative, exciting, vs. all assignments and work.

    c. Time: Task time, reflection time, breaks.

    d. Appropriate sequencing.

7. **Introduction** - get their attention, introduce yourself (if time and appropriate, have them introduce themselves). Explain format and obtain interest/excitement.

8. **Body** - Present concepts, skills, awareness.

9. **Conclusion** - What they've learned, what they can use tomorrow, what they can use later, how to retain the information, etc.

   a. **Skill Complexity**: Easy, Difficult, In-between?

   b. **Risk factor** to participants: Light? Heavy?

   c. **Practice**: Instructor demonstration? Class participation?

   d. **Atmosphere** conducive to learning: Comfortable surroundings, attitude of instructor etc.

   e. **Variety**: Lecture, PowerPoint, overheads. media used, length of segments, activity.

   f. **Method of Instruction**: (covered later)

   g. **Intensity of Training**: High? Low?

   h. **Costs:**

10. **Evaluate and validate training.**

    Evaluation: Relates to the methods used in learning during the training. Determine this with the use of tests and follow-up to see if trainees have learned what was taught. This can be done at the end of training or as late as a year later. This is done in class or on-the-job and will use several measuring devices, (how it affected the people involved etc.)

    Validation of Training: Relates to the course content of the training session. Was it geared towards reaching the learning objectives? If not - the training wasn't valid and was a waste of training time and effort.

188

Tangible/intangible behaviour:

When identifying objectives of training, use only tangible behaviours:

Tangible: Measurable and objective such as:

At the end of training, participants will be able to:

Write; recite; identify; differentiate; find; solve; construct; list; show; conduct; demonstrate; choose; express; state; explain; give; define; relate; determine; describe; present; evaluate.

Intangible: Hard to measure and subjective such as:

At the end of the training, participants will be able to:

Understand; remember; recognise; be aware of; perceive; appreciate; knowledge of; know; comprehend; be familiar with; realise; be acquainted with.

You will see that the intangible ones would be difficult to measure. Use only tangible and measurable words when setting objectives.

Setting objectives:

To put the training picture in perspective, you will determine the following:

a) Tangible behaviour: Using action words, which describe something you can observe them, doing.
b) Conditions: Explains your method of training and when you expect training to be effective.
c) Minimal Level of Achievement: Usually quantity, quality and time

Here are sample objectives from my *Train the Trainer* seminar:

Objectives of Learning:

General: Participants will learn how to prepare and present training programs to meet specific training needs of adult learners.

189

Specific: (Conditions and minimal level of achievement)

At the end of the seminar, by examining presented information, through discussion, group activities, self-study, assignments, training films and practice lecture, participants should be able to:

(Tangible Behaviour)

- Describe 19 qualities of a good training facilitator
- Relate 14 characteristics of adult learners
- Identify learner's needs through 13 training assessment methods
- Explain the meaning of the terms Training and Development and give an example of each
- Write 5 ingredients for setting training objectives
- Define tangible and intangible behaviour and give an example of each
- Show 13 methods of instruction
- Express the meaning of Theoretical and Practical training and where each is used
- Give the differences between Technical and Personal Growth training and give an example of each
- State the uses of 5 different training aids
- Recite 5 steps in the Training Procedure
- Demonstrate 2 kinds of training re-enforcement and give an example of each
- List 6 steps used in one-on-one training that are most effective for retention of information
- Differentiate the 8 steps in the communication process
- Define Paraphrasing and give one example of how it can be used in training
- Relate normal speaking and listening speeds
- Choose 2 methods of keeping participants motivated to learn
- Present 2 tips relating to what instructors should wear when training

Identifying costs of training:

You'll need to establish training costs to establish a budget. These expenses could be:

1. Room rental;
2. Handouts and overheads;
3. Refreshments and meals;
4. Man-hours of employees who are away from productive work;
5. Equipment rental – PowerPoint projector; video recorder and monitor; overhead projector and screen; slide projector; flip chart, blackboard or whiteboard; podium or microphone;
6. Cost of instructor/resource people - their fee, travelling expenses etc.;
7. Notepaper, pens, pencils, binders, name tags, etc.; and
8. Advertising, brochures, e-mails, etc. (if necessary).

Methods of Instruction:

There are many ways to train participants:

Multi-Media: Many trainers use this method. It uses role-plays, films, cases, lectures etc. and has the multi-media approach. The general idea is to bombard every sense and "ram" the message home to the participant. (This is my favourite).

Seminars/Workshops: You can accomplish a lot by these one- or two-day sessions. This rapid orientation is especially effective with an audience that's alert, interested and anxious to learn.

Simulation: Includes such techniques as role-playing, business, and other games (computerised or manual). It has the same advantages mentioned for case discussions.

Theory/Practical/Example/Lecture: This is where a trainer explains a complicated theory and gives a practical application of the theory. The trainer then asks participants to give an example of how they could use the theory.

Lecture method: On the surface, it's one of the most efficient methods for imparting ideas. A lecturer in one hour can cover a large number of ideas and/or areas of instruction. Speed of coverage and efficiency is the advantage of the lecture method. Its disadvantage is that much of the lecturer's input can be lost because nothing in the participant's own experience can relate to the information. It's best used in combination with other methods.

Case Studies: Provides cases for participants to study and discuss has become a standard method. The advantage is strong involvement of participants and their own reactions. A disadvantage is the time consumed in writing a good case and in encouraging free and full participation and discussion.

Programmed Learning: These are "pre-packaged learning systems" or "canned sessions " The major drawbacks are that they're normally very expensive and become obsolete very quickly. A secondary problem is that the facilitator did not prepare the program and may not have enough knowledge to answer participant questions about the content.

Correspondence & Home Study: This method is inexpensive, convenient and can accomplish much. Its weakness is that it lacks immediate feedback and face-to-face contact. Learners require a high level of self-discipline.

Reading: Many training personnel insist that reading changes nothing. Many participants are as adamant that a good book or a good idea in a book has "changed their life." It does give a good basis if used as a pre-requisite to attending a seminar or as back-up for future use after a seminar.

Laboratory Training: This learning method helps participants analyse their own experiences and identifies other ways they could have handled situations better. Everyone in the group is encouraged to give their input.

Sensitivity Training: Teaches participants how their behaviour affects others and how they can adapt their present behaviour to be more acceptable to others.

Encounter Training: This is an adaptation of sensitivity training. It focuses on body movement, body touch and "internal feelings." Its major emphasis would seem to be on heightened awareness and enjoyment of feelings and emotions. This method may be very threatening to some participants.

Situational Training: This method usually begins with some formal program of training. The participants are in "family groups" that work and relate together on the job. Usually, an outside trainer helps them to begin the process. The "work group leader" takes on more and more of the training responsibility and uses on-going organisational problems as the learning vehicles. It is a learn-as-you-do process and one of the sought-after benefits is to learn how to handle similar future problems. This is also the case when a supervisor involves his/her staff in brainstorming to come up with the best solutions to problems.

Preparing for a seminar/workshop:

Before presenting a seminar, do the following:

1. Determine the training needs.
2. Make a list of objectives that will meet the training needs using tangible objectives.
3. Research the topic thoroughly.
4. Choose from your research the material what you wish to use.
5. Put into a semblance of order (a) (b) (c) so ideas flow. Provide comments that will bridge between similar areas of study.

6. Brainstorm to determine the best method of presenting the information to the group (through lecture, handouts, films, discussions etc.)
7. Choose which training aids you'll use. Be sure to preview films and that PowerPoint and overhead projectors, videocassettes, slide projector, etc. are all in working order.
8. Prepare a leader's guide.
9. Prepare handouts and overheads.
10. Work out timing for each segment - keeping in mind coffee and lunch breaks. (Remember the need for participants to move around occasionally).
11. Revise program as necessary.
12. Choose class size and room set-up best suited to the program.
13. Determine risk level for participants (group activities are less risky for participants - don't make risks too high at the beginning of the seminar).
14. Set the date for training (be careful choosing day of the week - mid-week seems to suit most people).
15. Have paper, pencils and folders or binders available for participants (optional).
16. Be at training area at least one-half hour before class starts. Make sure all equipment handouts, films etc. are there and in proper working order.
17. Conduct training session.
18. Evaluate and validate training.

Group vs. individual activities:

The risk factor to each individual increases when they have to speak in a classroom situation. Many participants will resist having to speak up in class to relate their experiences or ideas. Others may try to take over the class because they're too expressive in their comments and may dominate the group.

To bring out the quiet ones (using their nametags to identify them) call them by name and ask them for their opinion on the topic. Have different people be spokespersons in group activities.

To quiet down the loud ones - state, *"The class is making John do too much work. It's time to give him a break and for the rest of you to speak up."* In group participation sessions, encourage each participant to express his or her ideas - not just one person. Encourage different people to lead groups (especially the quiet ones).

A facilitator of a seminar must provide a climate of mutual trust, respect, and openness, focusing on the positives in themselves and others. In group activities, participants are encouraged to share their problems and fears. There they can gain from the knowledge and resources of others who have been in similar situations and faced similar problems.

Group activities decrease the personal risk factor for learners. It gives several important advantages over one-to-one or individual experiences. Participants find comfort in knowing others share similar difficulties. It's often heard *"I thought I was the only one with that problem!"*

When you divide participants into groups, have them appoint a spokesperson before discussing the topic. Each subsequent group activity has a new spokesperson. As the spokesperson is speaking for the group (not themselves) even the quieter ones will feel less threatened.

In situations where you're pushing for assertiveness in public speaking, have the spokesperson make his/her presentation at the front of the class. Occasionally provide a microphone to increase learning of this new skill.

Technical vs. life skills:

Technical Training:

Use variety in training to keep the interest of participants at technical training sessions. Technical skills range from how to fix your car to how to run your computer. Technical skill training usually involves more homework and more concentration on the part of the trainee. Many participants anticipate (and rightly so) there will be a test after the training. Therefore, the element of risk on the participant is higher. Examples of technical training given in the workplace are:

- Supervisory skills of any kind;
- Computer training;
- Product knowledge;
- Selling techniques;
- Problem solving and decision making;
- Employee discipline; and
- Employment interviewing.

Life Skill Training:

These are sessions that help a person grow in other than technical areas. Participants are likely to be more responsive and less threatened at life skills sessions. Examples of Life Skill training are:

- Interpersonal skills;
- Stress management;
- Time management;
- Assertiveness training; and
- Non-verbal communication.

Theoretical vs. practical training:

Theoretical:

- The analysis of a set of facts in their relation to one another.
- A plausible or scientifically acceptable general principle offered to explain phenomena.

Practical:

- Designed to supplement theoretical training by experience.

- Actively engaged in some course of action.

I use a mixture of the above methods. For example:

a)   I introduce a theory i.e., Maslow's Hierarchy of Needs.

b)   I give practical examples of the theory. i.e.: When training participants; it's an asset to know where they fit - what motivates them to learn. Is it a need:

   (i)   to obtain information to fulfill the obligations of their position which would allow them to put bread on the table (Physiological need) or,

   (ii)   is their job in jeopardy because, if they don't learn the information, they may lose their job (security need) or,

   (iii)   will they remain behind their peers if they don't obtain the needed information (social needs) or,

   (iv)   they may not obtain a promotion depending on whether they learn the information (ego needs).

c)   Have participants decide how this theory and practical application apply to their own specific situation or needs. They're encouraged to give examples of where and when they would use it.

Bridging:

Try to have one topic flow into another by bridging two topics. For example: If I was talking about the different methods I could use, I might bridge onto the topic of costs. I'd say, *"One thing to consider along with what method you choose is the cost of each method of training."* Then I'd bridge into explaining the importance of proper timing of training programs, etc.

Timing of training segments:

I've found that this is a trial-and-error area. You'll have to anticipate how much time to leave for class participation. This, by the way, is the most unpredictable area of instructing. If you have a quiet group, you may find your timing is all off. If you have a group who really gets into the discussion or (Heaven forbid) get a "loudmouth," you may find yourself running behind.

The first time I present a training program, I put estimated times in the margin of my leader's guide (in pencil). For instance - I'll write in the margin that a segment will run from 10:45 to 11:00 am. As I go through the first run-through, I write, "needs more time" or "took less time" which I implement for the next session. Soon I have a good idea of how much time I really need. The more proficient you become at presenting seminars, the better you'll become in this area.

Use of training aids:

Training aids are anything that you use to help your participants learn. For example:

- PowerPoint projector and computer;
- Audio-visual equipment;
- Video cassettes;
- Overhead projector;
- Slide projector;
- Flip charts, either prepared or blank with felt pens;
- Handouts/binders. Decide whether you'll give the handouts one at a time, all at once or in packages;
- Blackboard or whiteboard plus chalk and felt pens;
- Samples of forms or products;
- Gimmicks (to lock-in training); and/or
- Guest speakers/resource people.

Re-enforcement of training:

Participants want to know ahead of time what's being taught. Being able to measure personal progress increases the participant's motivation to learn and retain the training. They must use the training to retain it. Teaching an employee a new skill they won't use right away is a waste of training.

For example: Teaching an employee supervisory skills, when it's known that it may be a year until they're able to use the skills. In some cases, they're taught proper supervisory skills, but go back to an environment where their managers haven't had basic supervisory training. These managers balk at the "new ideas" their supervisors give them on how they should be doing things.

Make sure that the manager and supervisor receive the same kind of training if you perceive this training is lacking in the manager. Suggest that the managers "sit in" on the training session "so they can monitor how well the supervisors do when they return to work." This saves face for the manager and results in their receiving the necessary training.

How to keep participants motivated:

If your program has followed the suggestions I've made, you'll find that participants will stay motivated to learn. Watch your audience to see if you're losing them. Look for signs of restlessness, loss of eye contact, fewer questions, yawning. You can get them back by having them move around, give a stretch break, use a little humour. Try telling them they'll be having a test or give a change of pace.

Instructor's apparel:

Trainers should wear comfortable clothing and shoes suitable to the group being trained. Female trainers should not wear bold prints or stripes that are hard to watch for any length of time. Make sure your shoes are "worn in."

Presentation skills:

1. Are you projecting your voice properly? Should you be using a microphone for large groups? If so, what kind - on a podium, portable or clip-on? (Check for squeal or feedback).
2. When speaking in front of groups exaggerate your gestures.
3. If you walk while you speak - don't pace or turn your back to your audience.
4. Don't talk when showing PowerPoint slides, if participants are taking notes from it.
5. Watch for your nervous habits while presenting such as clicking a pen; hand in and out of jacket pocket; smoothing or stroking hair etc.
6. Use notes - don't rely on memory. You don't have to use them but have them ready in case you lose your train of thought.
7. Use humour occasionally to keep participants interested.
8. Watch your audience for attention level and understanding of what you're explaining.
9. Don't ramble on - be specific.
10. Make eye contact occasionally with members of your audience (short time only - 3 seconds maximum eye-to-eye contact).
11. Dress one level above your audience.
12. Don't use big words and use technical terms only when necessary.
13. When writing on flip chart - don't stand in front of it; stand to the side, so they can see what you're writing. Don't have your back to them - stand beside your flip chart.
14. A podium helps keep your notes out of sight. Don't; however, spend all your time behind a podium unless you are delivering a speech using a fixed microphone. Use a mobile clip-on microphone if possible.

15. Keep extra strips of masking tape handy. Use these for a multitude of reasons.
16. Have paper and pencil handy to jot down notes for follow-up especially after group discussions.
17. Have a wrap-up at the end of the seminar to review content of the seminar. Explain to participants that the training is only effective if it's used. Encourage them to follow-up on any areas identified during the session where they need improvement.

Methods I use:

The method I use most often is the multi-media method, especially for one-to-three-day seminars where people are in one place all the time. For active people, putting them in this kind of environment is not only uncomfortable, but not conducive to learning. Therefore, I must provide variety and movement of the participants to meet this need.

I use lecture, films, overhead projector, PowerPoint, handouts, role-plays, case studies, group and individual activities and discussion periods.

I ask three questions at the end of the seminar. The participants answer them and pass them in (anonymous information). These three questions are:

1. How well did this seminar meet your particular needs?
2. How could I improve this seminar for the next group?
3. What is the most significant thing you learned today?

Now that you know how to put together and present training seminars, it's time to concentrate on improving your Meeting Skills.

CHAPTER NINE

MEETING SKILLS

The most important person at a meeting is the facilitator or chairperson. His/her main functions are to:

- Keep things running smoothly;
- Keep participants motivated; and
- Get things done.

Smoothly run meetings are a rarity. For instance, you chair a meeting, delegate assignments to your group, have a follow-up meeting and get these comments:

1. *"I didn't know I was responsible for that?"*
2. *"I didn't agree to do that!"*
3. *"I thought you didn't need that till next week!"*

You should have:

a) Planned your meeting;
b) Prepared for your meeting;
c) Known how to chair a meeting;
d) Understood meeting traps; and
e) Know how to handle problem participants.

Groups don't function properly without a formal or informal leader. One of the measures of your success at chairing a meeting is your ability to lead others.

Conducting meetings:

Supervisors may hold weekly or monthly meetings with their staff (normally held in their own facility). Other times, supervisors may hold informal meetings on-site (at field sites) where the employees complete their tasks. Or they may be called upon to chair a meeting that includes supervisors from other offices, branches, or cities. These meetings may be held in a meeting room of a hotel, in the boardroom of another company or in their own facilities.

Therefore, supervisors need to understand how to chair meetings properly so they can attain the desired results.

Role of the chairperson:

The chairperson's role in any group situation is to help achieve the objectives defined for the meeting. Other functions include:

Planning a meeting:

Planning for a meeting usually is done in the form of an agenda that may or may not have input from meeting members. The planning will include deciding where and when to hold the meeting, what will be discussed and by whom and ordering the necessary audio-visual equipment. A copy of this agenda will be sent to all participants so they can bring the necessary documents and information to the meeting.

During the meeting, the leader should consider how to deal with such situations as:

1. Is the group moving towards meeting the objectives?
2. Are individual needs being met, as well as group needs?
3. Is the meeting climate psychologically conducive for changes to take place?
4. Are participants working harmoniously with each other?

Use and develop group's unique talents and abilities:

- If members of the meeting are your subordinates, check their personnel files to determine their areas of expertise. One may be an exceptional organiser so you'd delegate things that would bring out this talent. However, if you aren't aware of this skill, you may delegate the responsibility to a less qualified member.

- If you don't have access to personnel files (possibly person works for another department or company) ask them to volunteer for tasks they can handle.

- At meetings, try to provide an atmosphere that shows people they're important. Don't interrupt - listen to what they have to say. Occasionally, you'll have to reject ideas. When rejecting ideas, you need to explain why. Make sure members know you're rejecting their idea, not them. Do this by encouraging further input and ideas from them. Never label people in any way i.e. *"How dumb can you be! We've tried that twice before and it didn't work."*

- Encourage an atmosphere conducive to change. Show them you encourage new ideas and ways of doing things. Bring out their creativity.

- Use "brainstorming sessions" when tackling problems. Encourage a free-wheeling atmosphere that encourages new, innovative ideas. This process enables you to have Plan B and C on the back burner if Plan A doesn't work.

- If participants stray off topic, bring them back with such statements as *"We're getting off track. We were discussing ... Does anyone have an idea?"*

Overcome cultural or personality differences:

If a personality clash happens at a meeting, stop the members involved. Arrange for a meeting later with the people involved so you can discuss the problems identified by the clash. Then bring the group back on track by suggesting, *"Let's get back to the topic we were discussing. I need all of you to concentrate on reaching the objectives of this meeting."*

If the leader is dealing with people of different cultural backgrounds, it's important that s/he understands what makes that person tick. Discourage any discrimination shown towards meeting participants. Jokes at the expense of someone else are not jokes at all. Discourage such discriminatory comments by stating, *"I didn't think that was funny, Paul."*

If Paul states, *"I was only kidding."* reply, *"Paul, your comments were a put-down to Harry. If your comments are as harmless as you say they are, then they're pointless and a waste of time. Keep these kinds of comments to yourself."*

Evaluate:

The leader must constantly assess the feelings of the group, as well as the group's progress toward accomplishing the task. The chairperson may have to table some issues for a later meeting, because crucial information was not available.

Follow-up:

Make sure members are aware of what they're to do and follow up. It's fine to decide that Peter will oversee doing something, but if Peter doesn't do what he says - the meeting won't accomplish all its objectives.

Before the meeting adjourns, ask each person to relate what s/he has to do towards reaching your team objectives. Then state, *"Peter, can I count on you to do ...?"* After the meeting, send each member a copy of the minutes of the meeting that includes information about delegated tasks.

Note: ***Learning to Work in Groups*** by Matthew B. Miles is an excellent book about meeting skills.

Preparing for a Meeting:

1. Set specific goals for the meeting. Know what you want to accomplish and when.
2. Determine what decisions must be made at the meeting and those that can wait.
3. Establish time frames for each topic on the agenda.

206

4. Set up plans of action to deal with #2.
5. Decide who will attend the meeting. Delete any that cannot benefit or give assistance at the meeting. Expect and encourage everyone to participate fully.
6. Prepare an agenda and distribute to those invited to attend the meeting.
7. Contact participants and explain what part they'll play in the meeting (what you want from them). Make sure they're able to attend the meeting or will send a knowledgeable person in their place.
8. Choose a time and place that's most suitable to the attendees. The physical surroundings affect the atmosphere of the meeting. For instance, the temperature of the room, seating and involvement of members. Remember access to the room (wheelchairs?) its size, preferably movable furniture, the acoustics, lighting and whether or not there are adequate parking and rest room facilities.
9. Arrange to have someone available to take notes and get refreshments. (Don't assume that one of the female members should do this).
10. Anticipate
    a) Costs;
    b) Problems (i.e. crucial members can't come to the meeting);
    c) Objections (legitimate or otherwise);
    d) Arguments (regarding the necessity of your goal. Have facts available to back up your idea);
    e) Personality problems that might surface between participants attending the meeting.
11. Prepare handouts and other back-up material essential for the meeting. Have facts, not assumptions to back up your ideas. Use a little showmanship by making your presentations interesting and informative. Use PowerPoint presentations, overheads, flip charts, computer printouts,

anything that makes what you're discussing clearer to the participants.

12. Make up name cards for the tables, so people can address others by name. (Not required when attendees know each other).

13. Smoking has become a very touchy subject. Consider the comfort of all participants and decide whether this will be allowed at the meeting, at coffee breaks or not at all. My research proves that this is one of the pet peeves of non-smokers. They resent being forced to attend meetings where they have no choice but to sit in a smoky room. Those with allergies may have traumatic physical reactions. Try to allow smokers adequate "smoke breaks" away from the meeting room if allowed in the building.

14. Discourage outside interruptions. Ask participants to turn off their mobile phones and have messages taken for them unless they are emergency situations. Try to have the meeting place away from the normal work setting to discourage this.

Avoiding planning blunders:

1. Meeting planners often plan with no data about the participants, nor their hopes and expectations about the purpose of the meeting.

2. If you're planning a meeting, identify:
   - Who's coming;
   - Why they're coming; and
   - What specifically is to be accomplished at the meeting?

3. Lack of involvement in the planning by those who'll be at the meeting. When you don't involve participants in some direct way, they'll probably not take an active part or may not even come to the meeting. They probably feel they'll be wasting their time attending the meeting.

4. Beautiful, but illegible visual aids. You may find that your visual aids are visually pleasing, but you may find that when you try them out in a large room, you can't see them.

Check all your visual aids in the room where they'll be used. Make sure that PowerPoint computer programs, video recorders and overhead projectors are in good working order and extra bulbs are available for projector.

5. Same meeting, same place, same time and objectives. Though sameness gives security to some, it bores others to tears. Why not vary the place and time of the meeting to suit different people in the group?

6. Holding meetings only because they're scheduled to be held. If there's no real reason or agenda for a meeting, why hold it? Can you imagine how motivated members would be if they could count on its being really meaty and full of content? They should know that if there's nothing to discuss you'll cancel it.

7. Lack of plans if extra people turn up. Often meetings planned for 50, have 75 or 100 people attend. Can the room be made cosier if the opposite happens and fewer people than were planned arrive? It's important to have some contingency plans.

8. No agenda or the one that omits the purposes for this particular meeting.

9. Too many items/activities planned for the time available. A realistic plan is needed to determine how much time various items or activities will take. If you have more items than the time allows then;

    - Cut out some items;
    - Increase the meeting time;
    - Arrange to put them in as pieces;
    - Work on in small groups during the meeting; or
    - Have two meetings.

The use of questions at meetings:

1. Overhead Question – are those you direct to everyone in the room - used to stimulate ideas. For instance: *"What can we do to reduce traffic problems in our parking lot?"*

2. Direct Question – are directed to a specific participant.
   For Instance: *"Do you have any ideas, Gerry?"*
3. Relay Question - participant asks a question of leader for opinion or information.
   For Instance: *"What do you think we should do?"*
   The leader relays to the rest of the group:
   "Let's hear from the rest of you." or *"What do you think, Gerry?"*
4. Reverse Question - question asked of the leader where participant already has an idea of what will work:
   For instance: (Question) *"What do you think we should do about the parking lot problem?"*
   (Leader) *"I'm not sure, what do you suggest?"*

Here are some questions and how they can be worked into a meeting:

Where used: To redirect the discussion.
How used: *"How do you feel about this new idea?"*
Tips on use: Repeat the question as you redirect it.

Where used: To avoid experting.
How used: *"What do the rest of you think about this?"*
Tips on use: Repeat the question as you redirect it.

Where used: To open discussion.
How used: *"We need to determine the cost of building a new parking lot."*
Tips on use: Plan specific questions that ask for input from participants.

Where used: To get agreement and acceptance.
How used: *"Does that express your idea?"* *"Can you give us an example of what you mean?"*
Tips on use: Probe for specifics. Ask for specific examples. Use paraphrasing.

Where used: To conclude the discussion.
How used: *"Are there any other points to be considered?"*
Tips on use: Then move on to the next topic.

Where used: To provoke thinking.
How used: *"What do you think of that idea?" "What are the advantages?" "What are the dangers?"*
Tips on use: Pause to allow time for thought.

Where used: To secure participation.
How used: *"Bill, what's your experience with this?"*
Tips on use: Have questions in reserve.

Where used: To guide discussion or bring it back on track.
How used: *"How does that relate to our topic? What point are we considering?"*
Tips on use: Build questions on previous responses.

How to chair a meeting:

Send a copy of your agenda to each person attending the session. Include information relating to what documentation, files or input you expect from each participant. Then proceed as follows:

1. **Open the meeting:**

   a. Put the group at ease with a cordial greeting.
   b. Have participants identify themselves - where they're from, who they work for, etc. – establish their credibility so their suggestions and input are heard (not necessary if participants know each other).
   c. State the purpose of the meeting - what objectives are expected.
   d. Identify the problems or ideas for discussion using common words so everyone at the meeting can understand your idea or problem. (A public speaking course might help in this area).
   e. Outline the content of the meeting.
   For instance: *"First we'll ... Then we'll ... There will be a coffee break at ..."*

2. **Present first problem or idea:**

   a. State the facts.

b. Ask questions, to overall group or directly to an individual or to more knowledgeable participants.

3. Conduct the discussion:

a. Encourage participation from *all* participants. If some aren't actively participating, ask them a direct question they can't answer with a *"yes"* or a *"no."*
b. Control the discussion - avoid personal feelings that could result in arguments.
c. Prevent anyone from monopolising the discussion.
d. Keep the discussion on track.
e. Analyse the progress of the discussion.
f. Use paraphrasing to confirm opinions expressed by others.

4. Summarise discussion:

a. Identify the highlights of the meeting.
b. Evaluate ideas, opinions and experiences.
c. Arrive at conclusions or solutions - what the meeting accomplished.
d. Decide on a plan of action - how to handle the problem or idea using group recommendations and/or decisions when applicable.

5. Present next problem or idea:

Follow above procedure until you have discussed all the items. Don't go on to another topic until the group has made a decision or follow-up meeting arranged for each item.

Note: Watch participant's (and your) body language. You'll be able to tell whether you're coming on too strongly, too softly and if your presentation is too boring to keep their attention. Make direct eye contact with as many people as you can so they feel included in the proceedings.

212

Stand up if you feel the need to appear more forceful. If you wish a more informal atmosphere, sit down. Listen to ideas. Be willing to change your mind.

Types of meetings:

There are two basic kinds of meetings:

Information meetings: To pass on information which the participants don't have.

1. State the purpose of the meeting and the major topic of discussion.
2. Provide information in as much detail as necessary for full understanding. Carefully explain background information.
3. Allow questions and feedback so the chairperson knows:

   a. Whether or not the participants understood the information; and
   b. How they accepted it. Participants have the opportunity of clarifying anything that's not clear to them. Summarise the major points covered and any issues that require clarification.

Discussion meetings: These are used:

a. To solve a problem or develop a plan of action.
b. To obtain ideas or suggestions which can be used later to make a decision or,
c. To make the best use of the ability and experience of personnel.

Follow these steps:

1. State the problem or idea.

2. Identify the extent of the participants' involvement to:
   (a) Solve the problem.
   (b) Make suggestions.
   (c) Formulate a plan upon which management can decide.

213

3. Generate ideas, discuss, evaluate and formulate a plan or reach a decision that represents the consensus of the participants.

4. Summarise meeting to:

   (a) Make certain everyone understands and agrees with decision

   (b) Make sure everyone knows what they're to do following the meeting, if you require such action. (Very important).

Meeting traps:

1. **The un-briefed resource person or speaker.**
   This person comes in and has no idea what you really wanted or what the group is like and gives the usual canned speech that's *always* given on that particular topic by that particular person.

2. **Agenda not shared.**
   There's only one copy of the agenda available and the chairperson has it. It's hard for participants/members to feel involved when they can't see and understand plans of the meeting.

3. **Formal, classroom-style seating**
   This is rows of chairs all facing the front. This gives the participants the non-verbal clue that all action and wisdom comes from the front of the room. It makes it difficult or impossible for them to participate actively.

4. **Meeting starts with nothing to do for early arrivers.**
   If you know that your meeting will have a raggedy start, plan something for the "early birds" to do, discuss or think about.

5. **Long introductions of speakers, consultants, helpers.**
   This usually produces psychological distance between them and the participants. Give a short, warm welcome instead of a long prologue. Often speakers have ideas on

214

how they would like you to introduce them. Some will want to introduce themselves.

6. **Long, drawn-out, windy speakers.**
   Often people go longer than the limits they're given. It's important to go over the ground rules with them at the beginning of the meeting. You might introduce the speaker and say, *"The time of the following presentation is 12 minutes."*

7. **Total reliance on the one expert at the meeting**, rather than using that person to help uncork the resources of all the participants.

8. **Coffee breaks too long or short.**
   If too long, they may disrupt the continuity. Consider having water, coffee, tea and juice available throughout the meeting with just a short bathroom break if the meeting goes over two and a half hours. You may decide that coffee break is too short, which may not give participants the opportunity of getting to know fellow meeting participants.

9. **Failure to deal with feelings of participants.**
   Often groups are so task-oriented that they skip even everyday manners and may appear abrupt. For example: some people have excellent ideas, but shyness holds them back from offering them because of the atmosphere. Leader must ask direct questions to this person to obtain their active participation.

10. **No record of what happened at a meeting.**
    It's important that someone takes notes and documents meetings. These then become a history of those meetings, which defines plans, as well as decisions and commitments made by participants. Copies of these minutes are given to each person who attended the meeting.

11. **Follow-up.**

Neglecting to carry the group "into the future" to guarantee that the work of the meeting will pay off. i.e.: Be sure to decide who will do what and when and obtain commitments from them that they will do what they said they would do.

Dealing with problem participants at meetings

Participant is: Overly talkative - to the extent that other participants do not have an opportunity to contribute.
Participant may be: An 'eager beaver,' exceptionally well informed; naturally wordy or nervous.
What to do: Interrupt *with 'That's an interesting point ... Let's see what everyone else thinks.'* Directly call on others. Suggest *'Let's put others to work.'* When the person stops for a breath, thank him or her, restate the pertinent points and move on.

Participant is: Engaging in side conversations with others in the group.
Participant may be: Talking about something related to the discussion; discussing a personal matter or uninterested in the topic under discussion.
What to do: Direct a question to the person. Restate the last idea or suggestion expressed by the group and ask for the person's opinion.

Participant is: Argumentative – to the extent that others' ideas or opinions are rejected, or others are treated unfairly.
Participant may be: Seriously upset about the issue under discussion; upset by personal or job problems; intolerant of others; lacking in empathy or a negative thinker.
What to do: Keep your temper in check. Try to find some merit in what's said, get the group to see it too; then move on to something else. Talk to the person privately and point out what his or her actions are doing to the rest of the group. Try to gain the person's cooperation. Encourage the person to concentrate on positives, not negatives.

Participant is: Unable to express self so that everyone understands.

Participant may be: Nervous, shy, excited or not used to participating in discussions.

What to do: Rephrase, restating what the person said, asking for confirmation of accuracy. Allow the person ample time to express his or herself. Help the person along without being condescending.

Participant is: Always seeking approval.

Participant may be: Looking for advice; trying to get leader to support his or her point of view; or trying to put leader on the spot.

What to do: Avoid taking sides, especially if the group will be unduly influenced by your point of view.

Participant is: Bickering with other participants.

Participant may be: Carrying on an old grudge or feeling very strongly about the issue.

What to do: Emphasise points of agreement, minimise points of disagreement. Direct participants' attention to the objectives of the meeting. Mention time limits of the meeting. Ask participants to shelve the issue for the moment.

Participant is: Too quiet, unwilling to contribute.

Participant may be: Bored, indifferent, timid, insecure; more knowledgeable or experienced than the rest of the group.

What to do: Direct questions to the person that you're fairly sure s/he can respond to. Capitalise on the person's knowledge or experience by using him/her as a resource person.

Participant is: Seeking attention.

Participant may be: Feeling inferior or hiding a lack of knowledge by clowning around.

What to do: Keep reminding the person about the topic being discussed. Talk to the person privately. Point out what his or her actions are doing to the rest of the group.

Participant is: Uninvolved and unwilling to commit to new tasks.

Participant may be: Lazy; too busy already or feeling s/he should not have been asked to the meeting in the first place.

What to do: Ask for facts concerning the person's schedule. Ask the person to volunteer for tasks (others in group must as well). Make sure you ask the right people to future meetings.

Participant is: Already too over-committed to other things to take on new tasks.

Participant may be: Unaware of own skills and abilities or lacking in organisational skills.

What to do: Ask for facts concerning the person's schedule. Ask the person whether s/he is already over-committed. Tell the person you're counting on him or her. Send the person to a time-management seminar.

Participant is: A buck-passer who blames others for anything negative that happens and doesn't accept new tasks readily.

Participant may be: Unable to admit to making mistakes or afraid to take risks.

What to do: Make the person account for his or her actions. Ask for facts to back up allegations. Privately ask why the person won't accept new tasks.

Now that you know how to conduct productive meetings, it's time to learn how to put everything together so you'll be able to succeed as a supervisor.

CONCLUSION

Putting it all together

By now you will have:

- More clearly defined your role as a supervisor;
- Determined many more leadership styles you can use;
- Learned how to delegate and motivate your staff;
- Perfected time management techniques to make the best use of your and your staff's time;
- Learned how to solve problems and make decisions;
- Improved your interpersonal skills;
- Decided how to train and develop your staff so you can use their innate skills and abilities; and
- Learned how to conduct effective meetings.

Using the tools and techniques in this book, you're now prepared to take over your duties as a supervisor. In order to make these techniques work, you need to make a conscious effort to follow-through with what you've learned.

If you've done nothing else but realise that you've been doing things correctly, then this book has done what I wanted it to do. Somehow just knowing that what you're doing is right, can result in a raised self-confidence level that will be reflected by the increased respect you receive from your staff.

If you're having problems hiring the right person for the job, have a high level of employee turnover or have problems disciplining your or firing staff, my book *Easy Come - Hard to Go, The Art of Hiring and Firing Employees* and *Human Resources at its best* are worth investigating.

219

BIBLIOGRAPHY

Allen, David, *Getting things Done: The art of stress-free productivity*, Penguin USA, 2010.

Betof, Edward & Harwood, Frederic, *Just Promoted! How to survive and thrive in your first 12 months as a manager*; McGraw-Hill, 2010.

Cava, Roberta: See list of her books at the front of this book.

Craig, R.L., *The ASTD Training and Development Handbook*; ASTD, 2013.

Fast, Julius, *Body Language*; M. Evans & Co. Inc. 2002.

Julie Morgenstern, *Time Management from the Inside Out;* Henry Holt, 2000; and *Organising from the Inside Out*; Owl Books, 2004.

Robins, Stephen, *Supervision Today*; Prentice Hall, 2009.

Rosner, Bob; Halcrow, Allen & Levins, Alan S., *The Boss's Survival Guide*; McGraw-Hill Professional, 2010.

www.ingramcontent.com/pod-product-compliance
Lightning Source LLC
Chambersburg PA
CBHW060547200326
41521CB00007B/515